LIKE Salt & Pepper

A MEMOIR BY **PEGGY KING**

Like Salt & Pepper, copyright © by Peggy King, 2010
we3kings@frontiernet.net

All rights reserved. This book or any portion thereof may not be reproduced or used in any manner whatsoever without the express written permission of the publisher except for the use of brief quotations in a book review.

Cover and interior design by Robin Black, www.BlackbirdCreative.biz

PROLOGUE

On her way to our wedding Steve's four year old niece, Ruth Helen, kept asking her mother what my name was. Finally Ruth Helen exclaimed, "I can remember Peggy now. Steve and Peggy—they go together like salt and pepper." We liked that!

God has blessed us with a very active, somewhat unusual life. Many have suggested that I share our story. It has been fun recording memories and remembering so many wonderful friends and experiences.

As an introduction to our story I would like to share a letter written by my brother, Tom, to Steve and I on our retirement from Mountain Jewels Ranch. He and his wife, Susie, have always been such an encouragement to us. Tom's letter is a good outline of our story.

August 3, 2006

Dear Steve and Peggy,

When I think back on your life together, there is one word that stands out. This word describes every ministry you have tackled, every challenge you have faced, and every victory you have experienced. When I speak about this word, you are often the first people I love to use as an illustration.

That word is Faith—risk taking, visionary faith. People with visionary faith are sometimes perceived as being foolish; however, when God builds on Biblical faith, those of us watching stand amazed.

When Randy was a baby you traveled from church to church telling of your vision to build a camp for Native American children in the wastelands of New Mexico. The ranch was only a plot of ground with a run-down house, but you had the vision and saw the potential which today stands as a monument of the faith of Steve and Peggy King—Broken Arrow Bible Ranch.

It was faith when you totally changed direction and began to pastor the church in Shingletown. The same teamwork that you demonstrated in New Mexico was translated to the work of a church. You led the church through a growing phase by your vision of what God could do, and today that church is still thriving and growing.

But I believe your greatest step of faith was when you saw the ranch in Little Valley and envisioned a home for men with disabilities. God seemed to bring together all of your gifts and passion for ranching, horses, serving, camping and pasturing in this new calling. You were able to look past the broken down buildings and overgrown ranch, and see the potential of what stands today as a demonstration of God's work through your faith. And it is exciting to see your faith in Doug and Heidi as they begin to have new dreams and vision for the Ranch. As a parent, I know how thrilled you are to see your legacy of faith.

When I think of your active faith, I am reminded of the farmer who was very proud of his farm, and what he had done through his hard work. Someone reminded him that he ought to give God the glory and the farmer said, "You should have seen this farm when God was working it alone." God doesn't need us of course, but he chooses those who have faith to work the land, bring it into submission and accomplish His dreams through our faith. God and us—what a team. You have demonstrated that through your vision and faith in his plans.

With love,
Your very proud brother and sister
Tom and Susie McKee

PART I

My Story

ONE

Childhood Years

The country was in the middle of World War II when I was born to Bill and Virginia McKee. They were living in Vallejo, California where my Dad was working at Westinghouse, repairing submarine engines. It was November 1943.

Dad was born in 1913 in Kansas to Emory and Jessie McKee. Jessie gave birth to ten children and only raised four (Orilla, Maurine, Lucile, and my Dad, William).

Dad was always called Bill.

A daughter, Janie, died on the operating table when she was only five years old.. The doctor thought she had appendicitis but she died before he found her appendix. A son, Winfred, died when he was 16 in the huge flu epidemic of 1918. Dad and Winfred were very close, making his death really hard on Dad. Dad remembers that the family was quarantined inside their home so he helped his dad put Winfred's body out a window to neighbors to be buried. Four babies died in infancy.

The McKee family eked out a living on a small farm in Kansas. They raised chickens and pigs, all their own vegetables and some fruit.

Dad spent a lot of his time in the boy scouts. Scouts helped him set goals. He worked hard and received the Eagle Scout award. Just after he graduated from high school his Uncle Virgil (who had been Dad's scout leader) told him he was moving his family to California. He explained to Dad that there was no future for him in Missouri and that he should go with them. So Dad made plans to head for California.

The rest of Dad's family said, "If you're going, we're all going." They packed up everything they could and headed out west. It was during the Great Depression. Everything that could fit was piled and tied all over their old car. They picnicked for all their meals and slept alongside the road at night.

Dad found a good job at the General Mills flour mill in Vallejo. He bought himself a home, stayed involved in scouts and was a leader of a troop of boys. He often took the boys on camping trips and other outings.

My Mom, Virginia, was born in 1920 to Dick and Betty Weller. They lived in the Bronx area of New York City. When she was two years old her family moved to Alameda, California where her Dad and his brother-in-law bought an auto shop and service station. They were also buying three homes next to the garage (one for each of their families and one for their mother, and their sister and brother who never married).

Mom has a lot of memories of those early days in Alameda. She and her cousin Dorothy, who lived next door, were only three months apart in age They had great times together.

One day, when their Dads were away for a few hours, the girls decided to help in the garage. Their Dads often painted cars for people That day the girls spotted a freshly painted red car. Noticing some cans of kerosene alongside the car they proceeded to cover the whole car with the kerosene. After realizing the damage they had done they ran to their Grandma's house and hid under her table. Reeking of kerosene, it did not take long for the culprits to be discovered. Needless to say, they were punished and banished from the garage for a long while.

When the depression hit Grandpa lost the business. He rented their home out for $7 a month and moved to Merced where some friends let them live in a little house on a small acreage. There they could at least raise vegetables, a few cows and chickens to feed their family that now numbered seven children.

Mom's memories of those years are sad. Grandpa hated farming and was not good at it. Everything was hard to get. Mom and her oldest brother, Dick, milked the eight cows and cared for the chickens. They ate a lot of rice and oatmeal that was given to them from the government. She remembers putting cardboard in their shoes when the soles got really thin. They went barefoot a lot.

The irrigation ditch behind their home was great for swimming on hot summer days.

After a few years on that little farm in Merced, Grandpa landed a job in Sacramento where they lived for a year. They were finally able to go back to their home in Alameda when Grandpa got a job working for the WPA.

My dad and mom met through his sister Lucile. Mom and Lucile commuted to San Francisco City College together from Alameda. Every school day they took the local train to the ferry station and then took the ferry across the San Francisco Bay to school.

One Saturday they decided to go together to a theatre to see a movie. Lucile brought her older brother, Bill, along. After the movie he asked Mom if she would like to go for a ride the next day. Mom thought that Lucile would be coming also and agreed to go for the ride. When she discovered that Lucile was not going to be with him she was ready to call and cancel the plans. Her dad told her that she could not do that. She had said she would go, so she had to.

Obviously, they had a wonderful time together. Just three months later, on May 19, 1939, they were married. Mom's parents traveled with them to Los Gatos where they were married by the pastor of the Christian Church in his home on a Friday evening.

Dad and Mom honeymooned at Brookdale Lodge in the Santa Cruz Mountains that weekend. Dad was back to work on Monday.

Dad was seven years older than Mom. He owned a home in Vallejo. They were living there when my brother, Tom was born on November 28, 1941.

Mom had a hard delivery with Tom and was in the hospital for two weeks. While she was in the hospital the Japanese bombed Pearl Harbor.

The bay area was blacked out at night for fear of being bombed. Mom remembers the nurses trying to care for the patients while it was pitch dark.

After Mom got home from the hospital, one night during a blackout Dad was warming a bottle for Tommy. There was a knock on the door from a policeman. He told Dad, "You'll have to turn your stove off. I could see the flame."

I was born two years later, November 9, 1943. The war was still going on.

During the war Dad bought war bonds with each of his checks. When the war was over he had saved enough money from the bonds and from the sale of his Vallejo home to buy a home and 10 acres in Los Gatos, California.

When Mom was young her family used to camp in the Santa Cruz mountains just above Los Gatos. She loved Los Gatos and so did Dad. That is where they were married and had dreamed of living.

Los Gatos sits where the Santa Clara Valley meets the lower slopes of the Santa Cruz mountains. It is a gorgeous setting.

Since the war was just over, two of Mom's brothers, Dick and Bob were released from military service and had time on their hands. They lived with us for awhile and helped Dad build a small home at the bottom of the hill. Dad divided the property and sold five acres with the original home.

We moved down to the bottom of the hill in the small two bedroom house, while Dad started building a larger three bedroom block home at the top of the remaining hill. He was working full time as a carpenter in San Jose. That was when building in the San Jose area was really starting to boom.

I still remember several things about life in the little house at the bottom of the hill. I remember Mom washing clothes in the basement with the wringer washing machine. We did not have a refrigerator yet, (just an ice box). I remember the ice man delivering big blocks of ice for the ice box. We had an outhouse when we first moved there and one night I went out there by myself and was scared to death when an owl hooted from a tree just above it.

Sometimes Mom would entertain Tom and me by doing pantomimes. She would put an Al Jolson record on our phonograph, dress up with an old hat and cane, pantomime the record and dance for us. Mom also read a lot of books and poems to us. One of our favorites was "The Cremation of Sam McGee".

About once a year my great Aunt Millie would come to visit for a week or two. She was an old maid and was really a character. She was a short plump little lady, almost blind and very hard of hearing. She wore one of those old hearing aids that had a cord from the earpiece to the hearing unit she kept in a pocket. It whistled a lot. She was a fabulous story teller and made up exciting stories. My favorites were the ones about gypsies. Tom and I sat cuddled up to her on the couch enthralled with her tales.

In the spring and summer evenings and every Saturday, Dad worked on the big block home he was constructing for us at the top of the hill. Many times my uncles Bob and Glen stayed with us and helped on the house. Mom's sister Beverly lived with us for awhile when we were in that little house.

The new home had three large bedrooms, a huge living room and dining room and a big kitchen. Working on his off hours, it took Dad about two years to build it.

We moved to the big house when I was six years old. My Uncle Dick and Aunt Nancy rented the small home at the bottom of the hill while they built a home not too far away. Later Dad tore the little home down.

Tom and I had a great time living on the top of the hill. Tom would build go carts that we sat on and steered with our feet as we raced down the hill. One of my favorite memories was swinging on a big rope swing that Tom and I had on a huge eucalyptus tree. We also had a fort up in that tree. Dad made me a big play house in the yard that I really enjoyed. Tom was often working on a project with Dad's tools in the garage.

There was a creek at the bottom of the hill that I loved to play in. I would go wading and catch polliwogs and frogs. I kept them in a jar in my room. It was great fun to watch them grow legs, lose their tails and become frogs.

It was the late 40's and early 50's. Times were changing fast.

We got our first telephone. The phone would ring with either one long ring, two short rings, or three short rings. We only answered when it rang two short rings. The other rings were for the neighbors and if you were nosy you could hear their conversations. Of course, that was a "no, no" and very bad manners. Dad and Mom were strict with us and for that I have always been thankful.

We purchased our first automatic washing machine.

Finally we were able to get our first television. It had a black and white picture and a twelve inch screen. Our favorite programs were Roy Rogers, Hopalong Cassidy, and Howdy Doody. Tom loved to watch the Golden Gate playhouse on summer afternoons. It was a rule in our home that the television could not go on until after 3:00 p.m. Now that is a rule in our home.

When we first moved to Los Gatos my parents were a part of a small group of people who decided to start a church. They called it Calvary Baptist. Years later the name was changed to Calvary Church.

One of the members had a large home and invited the church to meet in their basement. My Dad was appointed the Sunday School Superintendent. They quickly filled up the basement so purchased 10 acres of land in Los Gatos and started building. It soon became one of the fastest growing churches in the whole state of California. In just a few years the Sunday School was running around 800 people. Dad was hired as a full time Christian Education Director and stayed on the staff until he retired 30 years later. Calvary Church, Los Gatos holds a lot of special memories for me.

One day, after a Vacation Bible School, Tom and I were playing church. He was the preacher and I was the congregation. He preached a very simple salvation message to me and then gave an invitation to accept Jesus as my Savior. I told him very truthfully that I wanted to ask Jesus into my heart. I guess we should have realized then that Tom was destined to be a preacher.

My best buddy was my cousin, Faith, who shared my bedroom for quite a few years. Faith's parents were missionaries in Tijuana, Mexico. Tijuana was definitely not a good place for a young girl to live and attend school. I was delighted that she was able to live with us. Even though she was seven years older than I was, we were very close.

My dad taught her how to drive when she was 16 and later when she was in nursing school he helped her get her own car. She and I had great times taking drives in the Santa Cruz mountains on Saturday afternoons. We would find interesting homes on narrow winding roads and then make up stories of the folk who lived in them. Sometimes we would go to the high school tennis courts and play tennis. It was definitely a game of hit and chase, but we had fun.

Tom, Faith and I occasionally slept outside under the stars in the summer. I'll always remember one night when we were sleeping outside.

Peggy's cousin Faith, who shared her room for years, graduation from Wheaton College, 1951.

We slept on the floor of what was going to be Tom's new bedroom. It was an addition to our garage and Dad only had the foundation and the sub floor constructed. The sub floor had some big knot holes in it. We had thrown thin mattresses on the floor for our sleeping bags. When we weren't looking, Tom had tied a rope to the bottom of Faith's mattress and put the rope through a knothole under her bed to come back up through a knothole alongside him. In the night he started pulling on the rope. Faith panicked and jumped out of her bag screaming, "There's something under my bed!" That was just the reaction he wanted!

Our hill had a prune orchard on both sides. Every August when the prunes were ripe, Mom Faith, Tom and I would pick prunes during the day. Dad would help in the evenings and Saturdays. We would load buckets and then tote them up to the boxes. It took three buckets to fill a box. Dad would pay us twenty five cents for each box we filled. I made $3.75 the summer I was 8 years old. I thought I was rich!

The last few years we lived there Dad hired other folk to do the picking.

Tom and I rode a school bus about five miles to school. We walked about one half a mile to the bus. It was a nice walk until I had to lug my books, lunch and French horn or violin.

My favorite friend from kindergarten to the third grade was a little Hispanic girl named Dora. Her family worked in the fruit.

When I was in the fourth grade another school (Quito School) was built closer to our home. We still rode the school bus but not as far. At Quito School my favorite friend was Medori, a Japanese girl, whose parents had acres of strawberries. Medori and I both played the violin. One year Medori and I went to San Francisco on a school bus, with a lot of older students from the school district, for a competition. We both won blue ribbons.

For several summers Mom signed Tom and I up to attend a two week music school that was put on by our school district. At the school we were able to play more than one instrument. Tom played the trumpet and took up guitar. I played the violin as my main instrument and started playing the French horn. In the eighth grade I was able to play the French horn in the San Jose Junior Symphony. Tom became an excellent guitarist.

Music became a very important part of our lives. I started private piano lessons in the fifth grade and began playing the piano for our church youth group in junior high school. As soon as I got home from school I would play the piano.

My grandpa gave me an old saxophone that I found in his attic. I had a lot of fun teaching myself to play that. A friend of mine, Judy, played the sax. We worked up a saxophone duet and entered a Youth for Christ competition in San Jose and received first place. The prize was a free trip to Hume Lake Conference Center in the Sierras for a week of YFC camp.

In high school I sang a lot in a trio made up of good friends, Jan, Darali, and myself. We enjoyed singing together and also enjoyed some really good times. Jan's Dad, Bill MacDougal, was our church's music pastor. He had sung for years in the Old Fashioned Revival Hour Quartet. He coached us and it was great to get a little voice training from him. We often sang for church (which had gotten quite large by then) and Youth for Christ. Darali had a little convertible sports car that we had a lot of fun in.

Tom sang in a quartet with three of his friends and accompanied them with his guitar. They were very good and also sang a lot for the church and Youth for Christ.

Private music lessons were expensive and so was living in the country. We were miles from my Dad's work at the church. My Mom went to work to help with these expenses. My parents many times fought off headaches, sore throats, fevers and flu symptoms to fulfill their obligations at work. Tom and I learned from them how to be responsible and that life can go on even with a few aches and pains. One had to be really sick to lie around at our house.

As a family we did a lot of camping. Dad, having spent so many years as a scout, loved to camp and so did Mom. Since Dad's birthday was on Memorial Day, we spent every Memorial Day Weekend camping at Yosemite National Park. Yosemite was always gorgeous that time of year. All of the waterfalls were full. The fire falls that they had over Half Dome each evening were really special. We often rented bicycles and rode around the campground roads and bike trails. We did a lot of hiking.

My favorite camping memory is quietly singing as a family around the campfire at night. Dad taught us a lot of campfire songs that he learned as a boy scout. Tom and I would harmonize and Mom and Faith were good sopranos. Tom accompanied on his guitar.

Dad helped with the Boys Brigade Program for the boys at church and Mom was a leader in Pioneer Girls. We really enjoyed these activities. I learned a lot from the badges and ranks I passed in Pioneer Girls.

For several years during the summer, the folks rented a cabin at Mount Hermon Conferences Grounds during the Biola Week. Biola is a college in southern California that provided a wonderful week of music and speakers. Dad would commute back and forth to work each day and was able to attend the evening meetings and spend the night with us. While Mom was attending morning sessions, Tom and I would catch crawdads in the creeks and go hiking.

In the afternoons Mom would take us to swim in the pool. In the evenings we all attended the services together. The singing and meetings were enjoyable for all ages. They often had an exciting missionary film after the service.

My Grandpa Weller had a cabin in the Santa Cruz mountains which was only about twenty miles from our home. Back then a trip on that mountain road was not one we took often. The cars often overheated when climbing the mountain in the summer. But several times a year on a Friday evening or Saturday afternoon we would trek up there. Sometimes we would spend the night. Grandpa always had boxes of crackerjacks for us and marshmallows to roast around the campfire. He loved to sing with us and was an excellent harmonica player. If we were really lucky and my Aunt Beverly and Uncle Glen were there, they would take us to the Santa Cruz boardwalk and we would ride the merry go-round and roller coaster.

Faith loved horses and a few times she and I went to a stable and rented horses to ride. She loved it and I was petrified. I was always afraid of the horses. Little did I know that horses were to be a big part of my life in the future.

My mother loved to entertain. We often hosted the special speakers that came to our church. I did not realize back then the fantastic opportunity I had meeting these wonderful folk.

My Dad was very active in the Santa Clara County Sunday School Convention. He and Mom often went to State and National Conventions. One year the State Sunday School Convention was held at our church and Dad was in charge. He arranged for Dr. Howard Hendricks (who was then the President of Dallas Theological Seminary) to speak. Our family hosted him for the week. That was an awesome privilege. He was really fun to have.

Several times we had the Charles Green family stay in our home. They were missionaries to Argentina. Their oldest son, Steve Green, became a renown Christian soloist. They were a wonderful family and we always enjoyed them so much. One time they gave me a cute little stuffed llama for giving up my bed. I took that little llama to college with me.

Our family spent many hours a week at church. I was in the 5th grade when the church hired Dad full time. We were there as a family every

Peggy and her brother Tom in Los Gatos, spring of 1959.

Sunday (morning and evening) and every Wednesday evening. Dad was there every day but Saturday.

Just before my sophomore year in high school, the folks sold our home and acreage and purchased a home in Los Gatos so that we would be closer to the church.

Tom and I both were really happy about the move because finally we were able to attend school with our church friends. We had been in another school district. It was the first time we ever remembered living on a city street.

We moved right across the street from one of my good friends, Betty. My best friend was G'Ann (short for Gladys Ann).

G'Ann, Betty and I were part of a gang of about eight girls from church that hung around together. Often on Friday nights we had a slumber party at one of our homes. On Easter break we would rent a cabin for the week at a beach near Santa Cruz. One or two of our mothers would come to chaperone. We would spend our days sunning on the beach and riding the waves. In the evenings we would build a campfire near the ocean, roast marshmallows, and giggle and talk.

We dated guys from our large church youth group. Most of us had a steady boy friend. We would wear their block sweater and class ring. I went steady with Alan for a year. Alan and I met in the church orchestra. We had a great time together but mutually decided to break up when he joined the Navy.

The 50's was a great era to grow up in. We felt safe and life was good.

I did housework two afternoons a week after school and had several steady babysitting jobs. Dad taught me to drive as soon as I was able to get my permit at age 15 ½. We had a 1947 Plymouth that I learned to drive in. I was so short (4' 10") that Dad had to put blocks under the seat so I could see well out of the windows. When I got my license the man who tested me wrote "pillow "on the license where restrictions such as eyeglasses are indicated.

I had an experience between my sophomore and junior years of high school that would effect me forever after. A good friend, Gayle, and I were sent by our church (on a greyhound bus) to spend three weeks with Faith's parents (my Aunt Grace and Uncle Rexford) in Tiajuana, Mexico.

They lived in a tiny house on the California side of the border. Each day we would cross the border and visit with folk in Tiajuana.

I had never seen such poverty. A lot of folk actually lived in the dumps. They made homes right along the side of the dumps out of stuff that had been dumped . They were just hovels and families were living in them. Other homes were on city streets but they were also extremely poor compared to what was just across the border in California.

I remember visiting a lady lying on rags in a shack made of tarpaper from the dump. She had a brand new baby and several other children. I just could not believe such poverty existed.

My aunt and uncle had started a church in one of the really poor areas. We called on the people in their homes and had a Vacation Bible School while we were there.

I had taken two years of Spanish but I learned right away that I did not know much. They talked so fast I did not know where one word ended and the next begun. The people were so sweet and really encouraged me when I attempted to talk with them. By the end of the two weeks I was doing much better. But it really encouraged me to take two more years of Spanish.

Gayle and I each gave Bible lessons in Spanish to the kids. We really had to work to tell those stories in Spanish. It was good for us.

We both got really sick to our stomachs while we were there and each had to spend several days in bed. We picked up a miserable germ.

Uncle Rexford and Aunt Grace had two children, Rex, Jr. and Faith. Rex, Jr. had severe epilepsy. His head and face were terribly scarred from the many falls he had taken. There were patches on their walls from places where Rex's head had hit so hard he had put holes in them. Because of his many falls, he was slow thinking and speaking.

Gay and I played a lot of board games with him. He usually won.

Those two weeks impressed on me how difficult it can be to live with someone with a serious disability. I felt so sorry for Rex and his parents. He did not have a very fun life, being stuck in the house most of the time. He very seldom got out and did anything exciting. The situation was a real burden to Uncle Rexford and Aunt Grace because they did not know what they could do to make his life better.

The summer between my junior and senior years of high school, I worked for the San Jose School District in their library. I typed catalog cards, book pockets and cards and learned a lot about library. It was a great job and paid well.

That same summer my folks drove Tom and his best friend, Daryl and myself all the way to South Carolina to Bob Jones University. It was Tom's second year there. We visited Washington DC and Gettysburg. It was really a great trip.

During my senior year (remembering all the great times we had as a family at Mount Hermon enjoying the Biola Conferences) I decided to apply to Biola College and was accepted.

PART II

COLLEGE YEARS

The Biola dorm in downtown Los Angeles.

TWO

Venturing Out of the Nest

I'll never forget that first trip to college. It was September 1961. I took the train to Los Angeles and was really nervous about going all by myself. My seat number was by a man who talked the whole trip. He wanted to give me advice about being away from home for the first time. He talked about college and all sorts of things (including what guys would want to do on a date). I should have just told him I had an older brother and also had a steady boyfriend for a year. He was very strange and made me extremely uncomfortable. I was so happy when he got off of the train in Santa Barbara.

My cousin Faith and her husband, Dave, met me at the train station. They lived in southern California where Dave was a professor of psychology at USC. I was so happy to see them!

They took me to my dorm room in downtown Los Angeles. Back then (1961) most of the freshman students at Biola had to live in dormitories located at the Church of the Open Door on 5th and Hope streets. It was in the center of Los Angeles. For a country girl it was a real shock. My room was on the 12th floor! The room was quite small with an old bunk bed and really antique furniture. I loved it. My room mate, Carol, and I had fun fixing it up. I really enjoyed all the girls on my floor.

The guys' dorm rooms were on the other side of the church. There was a four foot wall around the top of the buildings. We could see all over the city from up there and could lay out in the sun. We got there by cautiously climbing up the fire escape from the thirteenth floor.

The 9th through 13th floors of the dorm buildings were for Biola students. The lower floors were for church offices. Single elderly folk (mostly widows and widowers) lived on floors 6 through 8. The women were in our side of the building and men over on the guys side. They ate their meals with us in the basement of the church. We ate all our meals there on weekends and ate supper there every day.

A loud bell would ring and wake us up at 5:30 a.m. every Monday through Friday. We had to be on buses by 6:15 a.m. to catch the ride to the Biola Campus at La Mirada where we had breakfast at 7:15. Our classes started at 8:00 o'clock. After our morning classes we were given sack lunches to eat on the buses during the trip back to LA. My least favorite day was Wednesday. Every Wednesday we had cold meatloaf sandwiches. The meatloaf was leftover from dinner Tuesday night on campus.

We were the last class that lived in the downtown dorm. The next year there were enough dorms built at the new campus.

Living in that big old building was a lot of fun. We had many interesting experiences that would never have happened elsewhere. The worst part was that 5:30 a.m. bell.

Since I was a music major I had to practice the piano and the violin. Our practice rooms were in the basement of the building. All girls were required to take someone with us to check out our practice room before we practiced because bums were known to break into the windows from the street and sleep in the rooms. The windows were high in the room on the street level.

Only once did I find a bum in my practice room. He meandered out when we told him that we were sorry but he had to leave. I really wanted to tell him that I would only be a half an hour and after that I really did not care if he came back for a good warm place to sleep.

My best friend , Bev, was also a music major so we always went together and practiced in adjacent rooms. Bev had a beautiful voice.

Our laundry facilities were also in the basement. For exercise (we were gaining weight on the cafeteria food) we would see how many floors we could walk up before catching the elevator. Usually by the fifth or sixth floor we were ready to ride.

Bev and I got a job working at Clifton's Cafeteria on Friday nights and on Saturdays for the noon and supper meals. It was an old landmark cafeteria in downtown LA with a waterfall in the corner of the dining room. The bad part was walking home from the cafeteria at night. We had to walk through a really creepy part of the city called Pershing Square. A lot of really weird people hung out there. We walked very fast. The Lord had to have been watching over us because we never had any problems.

During Easter vacation I got a job running the elevator in our dorm building. (Most of the students had gone home for Easter break.) Dr. J. Vernon McGee (the renown Bible teacher and pastor of the Church of the Open Door) had his office on the 5th floor. I gave him many rides. He was a lot of fun! He always had a joke and kept me laughing.

There were some real advantages to living downtown. On Saturdays we could catch a city bus and go places. We went to Chinatown and Pacific Ocean Park . Of course, we always made sure there was a gang of us. I laugh now because we thought we were so smart—carrying hat pins to defend ourselves in case of trouble. We were going to poke any bad guys in the eye.

Every Biola student was required to have a Christian Service Assignment. That first year mine was teaching a Sunday School class of junior high school kids in the Watts area of LA. I thoroughly enjoyed it but the class was quite intimidating to this little country kid. The kids in my class were all bigger than me and they were all black. I rode to the class each Sunday morning with some upperclassman from the Biola campus. They would stop by and pick me up. I attended Church of the Open Door on Sunday evenings.

It was a great year. I was happy I would be moving to the new campus for my sophomore year but I am really glad that I had the downtown experience. I made a lot of unique memories!

There was about 200 students in our freshman class. In Bible Class (which met in the main auditorium) I sat right behind a guy named Steve King. He always wore cowboy boots. One of the first times I remember really noticing Steve was at a Biola soccer game where he did trick riding on a horse during halftime.

Steve was living with friends of his family who lived near the Biola campus. We chatted a lot in speech class (as there were only a few of us in the class). I thought he was really nice.

It was the end of our freshman year when he asked me to go to a concert that the Biola choir was performing. Since the performance was Sunday afternoon on the campus, he would not have time to attend his church near campus, then pick me up downtown and get us to the concert on time. So I invited him to attend the Church of the Open Door with me Sunday morning. And since he was in charge of the youth group at his church in the evening, I would have to go there with him. So my first date with Steve turned out to be 13 hours long. We got acquainted. And we both really liked each other!

Steve invited me to go with him the next Saturday to Griffith Park. It is a beautiful park in Los Angeles with lots of fascinating things to see. We had a great time. Just a few more dates and our freshman year was over.

I had a ride to Los Gatos with some students going north. Steve was heading up to his home in Bend, Oregon a few days later. He had another student, Suzanne, who was a couple of years older than us and from Bend, riding with him.

I invited them to stop by and visit me in Los Gatos on their way to Bend. It did not sound like they would come as they were both anxious to get home after a long school year. So I was once again very surprised to see Steve and Suzanne drive up our driveway a few days after I had returned home.

Steve and Suzanne spent the night at our house. Mom and Dad took us all to San Francisco the next day. We had a great time. That was the first time my folks met Steve. I remember my Dad telling me that he liked him. For me that meant a lot.

The last semester of my freshman year I started attending a missions prayer meeting that a good friend, Louise, encouraged me to attend. The group was organizing a team of students to work with the American Sunday School Union in Northern California that summer. They were going to run three weeks of camp and then hold three weeks of Bible Schools in the little communities around the Placerville area. It sounded like a great experience so I signed up to go.

The student who was in charge of the outreach, Jim, told me that he would come to my home and pick me up for the orientation week for the mission. It started just two weeks after school was out.

Our orientation was in the home of the American Sunday School Union missionaries in that area, Harvey and Pat Cowles. They had three children and a small three bedroom home. I was amazed how they added the seven of us into their tiny house. We studied lessons for both camp and Bible school and had a great time in prayer and Bible study.

One fun memory I have of that week was picking wild black berries in the woods by their home. One of the girls from our team loved making pies. She taught me how to make pie crust! I had never liked pies before, but I really liked those black berry pies.

Our weeks at Camp Forward were very interesting. I was used to big fancy camps (Hume Lake and Mount Hermon).

Camp Forward had rustic cabins with tent tops. The swimming pool was a muddy pond. Services were held outside on benches. There was a shelter over a small platform where the speaker spoke and the piano sat. The camp had a small kitchen in a cabin and we all ate outside. Fortunately we did not have rain.

Jim led the music and I accompanied on the piano at each service. Our speaker was Dr. Mow, who had been a missionary in the jungles of Borneo. He was fantastic. He held us all spellbound with his stories of Borneo. He was very challenging and also a lot of fun. We had a week each of junior camp, junior high camp and high school camp. Each week I had a group of nine or ten girls in a very rustic cabin.

After the three weeks of camp we divided up to go to small villages and run Bible Schools. Louise and I were a team.

Each week we went to a rural town and conducted a Bible School in some families' yard. Living in a different home each week was interesting.

The first week Louise and I were in the home of an elderly lady who was very fat. She spent her days in her wheel chair, and very seldom cleaned her house. We tried to help her but she did not want help. So we survived living in the mess. It was a memorable week

She had a parrot that talked a lot and was very loud. It was the first time I had ever experienced bed bugs. Half way through the first night we discovered we were both scratching! For the rest of the week we slept on top of our beds. The lady had a cow that the neighbor milked. She made her own butter, which tasted very rancid. After the first morning we ate our toast without butter.

We held a Bible School in her yard each day. There was a good turn out of neighborhood kids.

The next week we stayed with a very wealthy family. The man owned a John Deere Dealership and a large ranch. They had a very young girl and two teenage boys. Their home and the ranch were beautiful and neat as a pin. We felt like we had died and gone to heaven. We had Bible School in a little building that they held church in.

Our next Bible school was in a nice home in a mountain community. They had three teenage boys who were lots of fun. I particularly remember them taking us several times to a swimming hole that was in a canyon near their home. They had a rope swing that we would swing way out on and then drop into the water. It made me wish that some year I would be able to live in the mountains. And I thought living on a ranch would be great too!

I had two weeks at home before school started again. Steve and I corresponded a few times throughout the summer. He asked if he could pick me up on his way down from Bend. What a blessing! I did not to have to take the train!

THREE

STEVE'S STORY

On the trip to school Steve and I had a great time talking and we learned a lot more about each other. This year we both lived in the dorms on the Biola Campus. We met for meals each day. My Christian service assignment that year was helping in a Pioneer Girls Club at the Evangelical Free Church in Fullerton. We both attended that church together on Sunday mornings. For his assignment Steve joined a men's choir that sang in nursing homes on Sunday afternoons.

After a few weeks we decided maybe we were getting too serious so we should break up. We tried that for a few weeks and then Steve asked me out again. After church on a Sunday evening we went to a park. We got on an old merry go round and went round and round. Steve says to this day that he got me dizzy and then "popped the question". He asked me if I would marry him and I exclaimed, " Yes!". We decided we needed to wait to marry until at least one of us had graduated because college expenses were so high . We had two and a half years to wait.

I was a Bible major and Steve was majoring in Christian Education. Biola still had a three year Bible Institute course. I inquired at the office and found out that I could switch to the Bible Institute and graduate the next

Steve and I going into my new Biola dorm in 1964.

year. So that is what I did. I went from a sophomore to a junior just like that. Now we only had one and a half years left!

Steve gave me an engagement ring for Christmas 1963. We had a fun engagement party at my home in Los Gatos between Christmas and New Years.

During Easter break Steve and I drove up to Bend, Oregon so I could meet Steve's family. I was so anxious to meet them. That trip was an experience we will never forget.

Steve had traded his big 1957 Oldsmobile in on a little 1958 BMW Isetta. Believe it or not, back then we thought that 37 cents a gallon for gas was just too expensive. He got over 50 miles to the gallon in that tiny little car, but we really gave up a lot of comfort. The whole front of the little car opened up to get in. It was very creepy when you looked through the back window and saw the bumper of a huge semi truck behind you. I felt like a little fly about to be stepped on by a huge elephant.

Our plans were to drive about half way up to Bend and stay overnight at a friends house. A U-joint on the little car broke just outside of the town of Chowchilla, California. We pushed the car into a service station. No one in the area had the part so Steve had to call for one to be sent to us by greyhound bus. It would arrive at that service station the next afternoon. We ended up spending the night and half the next day there in the yard of the service station with that tiny little car our headquarters.

We called our friends and told them that the car had broken and that we would not be able to come by their place. Then we decided to park the car under a light at the station. That way if anyone we knew stopped by that station (like other Biola students on their way home for Easter) they could see that I was asleep in the little side seat leaning against my window and that Steve was on his side. I did let him sit on top of my feet because it was sooo cold! Needless to say we did not get much sleep. And we never traveled again with out a couple of blankets and pillows (and food) in the car.

The next morning we hiked all over the area until the part finally arrived around noon. The nice folk at the service station helped us put it in. By mid afternoon we were off again.

It was snowing hard when we reached the Mt. Shasta area. We drove through snow all that night! Our heater had quit so we bundled up in everything we could find in our luggage that might warm us a little. It was still snowing when we made it to Bend early the next morning.

Steve's Mom said she never forgot how tired and cold I looked the first time she saw me. She took me into her arms and I just knew that I loved her. Steve's Dad came home for lunch and I felt the same about him. They were both so nice. No wonder Steve was such a sweetie!

There were some things that I was not prepared for. Steve had never told me that his parents did not have any teeth. Actually, Mom had just a few bottom teeth, but no teeth on top. Dad did not have any teeth. They did not have enough money to purchase false teeth. Once, years later, when Mom and I were talking, she related how a couple of times she had such a bad toothache (and no money for the dentist) that she got the pliers and pulled the tooth out herself. Several years after we were married they were able to purchase false teeth. They said they were really hard to get used to.

I was also surprised to find so many people living in such a tiny little two bedroom home. Steve's Mom and Dad had a very small bedroom. Steve's younger brothers, John, Paul and Rod shared a room that was made out of the laundry room. It was a small room just inside the back door. Dad had built a triple bunk attached to one wall. They had one dresser for the three of them and a rod in a corner for their hanging clothes.

I shared a bed with Steve's sister, Judi, in a very small bedroom. Judi was only a year younger than me and I thoroughly enjoyed her. She is a lot of fun. Judi was dating Delbert Friesen who was also attending Biola. His family had a ranch in Culver, Oregon.

(Judi and Del married a year after Steve and I, while Del was serving in the Vietnam war.) We had some great chats.

Dad King had hooked up their washing machine in the little center hall way. The home had a tiny living room (probably about 12' by 12') that had just enough room for the gas furnace (that the boys took turns sitting on) a couch, one living room chair and a small TV. We sat all over the floor and it was quite cozy. The kitchen was also very tiny. It had a small cooking area and room for a large table with eight chairs closely squeezed together.

Mom had the place fixed up really cute and it was as neat as a pin. I was amazed at her ability to keep that little home so spotless. With the snow and mud outside and all of us coming and going, she lived with the dust mop in her hands. Dad and the boys kept the yard immaculate.

Steve had built himself a bedroom out in the garage. (He had told me his bedroom was in the garage and I had pictured the one my Dad had added onto our garage for my brother). Their garage was just a shed with a dirt floor. For his bedroom floor Steve had put some plywood on a frame that he built on the ground in the corner of the shed. Then he constructed the four walls with plywood and stapled insulation to them inside. He had put in a small wood stove, his bed, a dresser and a bar for hanging clothes in a corner. He had a throw rug on the floor for décor. I was so proud of his ability to make do and be so content.

Mom King and Judi and I had some great chats. I thoroughly enjoyed them both.

I learned a lot of the history of Steve's family. Steve had shared a little with me but I was simply amazed at their story.

Steve's Dad, Vernon Virgil King, was born to Alva Curtis and Ethel Marguerite King in Aurora, West Virginia on April 6, 1912. Dad King had two sisters and a brother, Lloyd.

When Dad King was just a youngster the family moved west. His Dad, Alva, drove teams of horses in a mine in Colorado for awhile. Dad's sister, Yvonne, told me once about the time when she and her brothers, Lloyd and Vernon, were all three riding a horse together. She being the youngest was on the very back. The horse reared and they all slid off and landed on a cactus with her being on the bottom.

Later they moved to southern California and lived in the Redondo Beach area. Alva was a stable hand and did a bit of training at the Palos Verdes riding stable for awhile. (Now I could see that Steve might actually have inherited this penchant he has for horses.)

Steve's Mom, Ruth Caroline, was born in Maine to Harold Sumner Farris and Myrtle Barnes Farris. Harold was a fisherman.

During World War I, Harold joined the navy. He was stationed in Long Beach and was a machinist. When the war was over he stayed in southern California and sent for his family.

He ran a service station in the Long Beach area.

Daughters, Muriel and Jean and son Harold Jr. (called Bud) were born in California.

Mom and Dad King attended different high schools. They met in a church youth group. They were married in Inglewood, California on April 30, 1933.

Six children were born to them while they were in California—Douglas, Harold, Janet, Priscilla (Pennie), Steven, and Judith. They decided that they wanted to get their family out of southern California and move to a smaller town. They lived in the Willamette Valley in Oregon for a short time and then moved up to Bend.

Dad King worked as a produce manager for a grocery store. He always worked six days a week and long hours each day to support his large family.

John and Paul were born in Bend, increasing their household to eight children. Often he was able to bring fruit or vegetables home that were getting too ripe. Mom would make a stew or soup that fed the family. She made great biscuits. She taught me how to add a can of corned beef to some white sauce and serve it over biscuits or mix the can of corned beef in with a bunch of mashed potatoes. With one can she would feed a crowd. Her tasty potato soup has always been a favorite at our home.

One of Steve's most vivid memories of his younger days in Bend was the day he froze his hands. He was in the first grade (6 years old) and the temperature fell to about 40 degrees below zero. School was let out early because of a storm. He walked home and had accidentally left his mittens at school. He would not put both hands in his pockets because he had a box of crayons in his hand that he was taking home for his little sister Judi. He fell a couple of times and got his hands wet. By the time he got home his hands were frozen. He remembers laying on the couch that night trying not to cry, but he had to cry. Mom said he put a hole in the couch from kicking in pain. A few days later all the skin pealed off his fingers like banana peels. His teacher felt so terrible because she did not realize he had headed home without his mittens. To this day he still has trouble with his hands aching in the cold.

Steve remembers Dad making him a wooden rocking horse that he called his Sammy horse. He really loved it. He spent a lot of time playing on that little horse, dreaming he was riding the trail.

They were members of the First Baptist Church. Dad did not have much time to attend as he usually worked on Sundays. Mom was there every Sunday with the kids and was busy in the ladies work. After most of the kids had grown and left home she worked part time for the church, cleaning bathrooms and the church offices. She kept them spotless.

For years they rented homes and moved often (whenever a more comfortable, affordable home was available to them). Mom was an excellent homemaker and always made her home look homey and cozy.

When Paul (their eighth child) was a baby they were finally able to buy a home. It was an old two story home on the outskirts of Bend. Steve remembers a large wood cook stove and the out house. He also remembers Dad lining up all the kids alongside the front yard to keep the sheep out when shepherds were driving large herds of sheep down their street to greener pastures on the other side of Bend.

They all really loved that big old house. Then one day Dad was out in the yard working in an old shed. He yanked out a corner cupboard that he did not realize was holding the whole shed together. The entire shed collapsed on top of him. When the neighbors helped to get him out, he was found with several breaks in both of his legs.

It was definitely going to be months before he could walk and the doctors were not sure that he would ever walk again.

Mom's parents (Grampy and Grammy Farris) lived on some acreage in Arkansas and had a small farm. They had an old empty cabin on the property and welcomed the family to live in the cabin.

So Dad and Mom packed up the five youngest kids and as much of their belongings that they could cram into their car and a trailer and headed for Arkansas. They had to send their oldest three children, Doug, Harold and Janet, on the bus. Dad drove that old car (with casts on both his legs) all the way from Oregon to Arkansas.

Grammy and Grampy Farris lived way out in the backwoods of northwestern Arkansas. Steve remembers riding to school in an old school bus. Most of the kids went to school barefoot.

Grampy said that he was not accepted with the neighbors when he first arrived. Then one day he went squirrel hunting. He fired three shots. On his way home he met some men who said, "We heard three shots." Grampy held up three squirrels. That evening the men came by their house to pay their respects. After that Grampy and Grammy felt like they were part of the community.

Steve loved it in Arkansas because Grampy had an old horse named Trixie that he let him ride. Steve loved helping Grampy care for Trixie. He spent hours with her. That was the first time he had a horse that he could ride.

The family of ten was crammed together in a small run down old cabin. Mom was getting very depressed with the whole situation.

The last straw was one day when she was hanging up the clothes (that she had washed on the old wringer outside) and almost stepped on a copper head snake.

As soon as Dad was able to walk. They headed back to Bend.

When they got as far as Ordway, Colorado their car broke down. They had stopped to visit some friends there. To get the car fixed Dad had to find work. He found a good job at the Ordnance Depot.

For a few weeks they stayed with their friends and finally found a small old cabin on a ranch that they could afford to rent. Steve remembers they moved a lot during that time in Colorado. They lived in Ordway, Crowley and Pueblo. Pennie says she remembers changing schools several times in one year. She found it very difficult to get a good friend that way.

Steve had a good friend, David Gray, from their church. His parents were ranchers. Steve spent a lot of time on their ranch and started dreaming of someday being a rancher. He loved it when Mr. Gray let him drive the tractor. The Grays also had some horses they let him ride. Steve enjoyed the time he spent in Colorado. Anytime he could be near a horse he was happy.

While he was living in Colorado, Steve made the decision that would direct his life from then on. It was a Sunday afternoon and the message at church that morning really spoke to him. He had some real questions about life and death so he questioned his oldest brother. Doug led Steve to the decision to be a Christian.

Rodney Dean (their ninth child) was born while the family was in Pueblo.

After three and a half years in Colorado, Dad and Mom were still homesick for Bend. So they packed up and headed back. With nine kids they were really crammed in their car. Each of the big kids had a little kid on their lap. Mom had the baby, Rod. Being the middle child, Steve was sometimes on the top and sometimes on the bottom.

Steve was in the fifth grade when they made the move back to Bend. He was glad to be back with friends at the First Baptist Church. They had a new pastor, Roy Austin. The Austins had a son, Roger, who was the same age as Steve and they lived on the same street for awhile. Steve and Roger became best buddies. The Austins were very good for Steve. He spent a lot of time in their home.

For awhile Steve lived near the big lumber mill in Bend. The mill still used draft horses for some of the logging. A man from the church, Frank Filey, was in charge of the horses. Steve would walk to the mill and watch Mr. Filey work the horses. He became a good friend and taught Steve a lot about driving horses and a lot about horses in general. Steve was in the horse barn at the mill every chance he could get. He often helped Mr. Filey harness the horses.

Steve also joined a riding club. The president of the club had an extra horse that he let Steve ride. He took a real interest in Steve and taught him a lot about good horsemanship.

Mom was scared to death. Steve remembers sneaking out of the house early in the morning to go riding. She was fine when he arrived home in one piece but if she was awake before he left she would beg him to stay home.

One time she agreed to let him go on a camping trip with the riding club. During the trip the horse he was riding leaped over a creek and Steve fell back on to the saddle with his wrist twisted under him. He broke it. He did not want to have to leave the ride so he tried to hide his pain. He would ride way ahead of everybody, get to the next creek, jump off of his horse and soak his wrist in the ice cold water. Finally one of the leaders realized what he was doing and looked at his arm. It was quite obviously broken so he had to leave the ride early, go to the doctor and get a cast on it. He felt worse about missing part of the trip than he did about the break. And he knew it would not help his Mom's fear.

Steve did not go on many trips as a child. Dad worked six days a week. Money was scarce. The family could not all fit in the car comfortably for a very long trip and Mom was very fearful of traveling. The only traveling Steve ever did was with the church youth group and one year in high school when he traveled with the football team. Mom worried the whole time he was gone.

It did not help Mom's fears when one time Dad and Mom were finally able to go on a trip by themselves to southern California. On their way they were hit head on by a young driver. Dad only suffered minor injuries but Mom's head went through the windshield and she was hospitalized for a few days. Her face required a lot of stitching.

Steve began working at Erikson's grocery store when he was a sophomore in high school. He usually worked with his dad in the produce department. He worked every Saturday, weekdays after school and full time during the summers.

Steve was always active in his church youth group. In high school he became very close to Fred and Ersa Westlake who led the group. Their son, Allen, was Steve's good friend. Steve spent a lot of time at their home. It was Fred and Ersa who encouraged Steve to go to college and helped him apply to Biola College.

When Steve applied to Biola, Fred and Steve's Pastor, Rev. Lunday, each wrote a letter to the college and encouraged them to accept Steve, even though he did not have high grades. His grades were average but low for being accepted to college. Biola did accept him.

Steve left for Biola in a 1950 ford he had purchased himself from money earned working at the grocery store. It was September 1961. Suzanne rode with him. When they reached the LA freeways they both just burst out laughing. They had never experienced anything like it! Masses of humanity-going in every direction!

FOUR

Courtship

So now we go back in this story to that Easter vacation when I met Steve's family for the first time. Learning Steve's history from his Mom and Judi, and meeting his family was so fascinating for me. It made me love and admire him even more.

Steve and I traveled back to Biola. This time we made an overnight stop at my home in Los Gatos. The weather was much better and we did not have any car trouble.

That summer (1963) Steve went with a group called Practical Missionary Training to the Navajo Reservation in Arizona and New Mexico. He spent one week with missionaries from the United Indian Mission in Supai Canyon (a tributary of the Grand Canyon). He also spent some time with missionaries in Window Rock. And he spent a week with missionaries, Charles and Iris Girton, on a mission station just south of Gallup, New Mexico. He helped run a week of Bible School there. Missions became very dear to his heart.

I spent the summer attending summer school at San Jose State. I took a US history course (that I needed to graduate) and typing and short hand. I was hoping that typing and short hand would help me get a good job after graduation to help put Steve through his last year of Biola.

Attending San Jose State that summer sure made me thankful for Biola. The San Jose State campus was huge and the students and professors were so different than I was used to. Steve had given me the little Isetta for the summer and I enjoyed driving it to school. It was easy to park and to maneuver around the busy San Jose streets.

My brother, Tom, had just become engaged to Susie Jackson (a girl he had met at Bob Jones University). Susie was from Lee's Summit, Missouri. We had never met her, so Mom and Dad decided it would be fun if all six of us could go camping at Yosemite.

Susie flew out from Missouri and stayed for a few days at our home in Los Gatos. She slept in my room and we had some great talks. (Susie and I are only a couple of months apart in age). Then we all drove to Merced and met Steve at a bus station. He was on his way home from his missions trip. From Merced we drove up to Yosemite (the six of us and all our camping gear in Dad's small car).

We talked over plans for weddings and graduations. The next summer my folks were going to have two graduations and two weddings in two weeks. Tom's graduation from BJU was the end of May. The following week he and Susie were getting married in Lee's Summit, Missouri. They were getting married on the same day that I was graduating from Biola. The next week in Los Gatos, Steve and I would be getting married. Susie and Tom were both going to be in our wedding.

What a great time we had! The camping trip was a fantastic way for us all to get better acquainted with Susie and Steve. We did a lot of hiking and sightseeing. Tom had his guitar so we sung around the campfire at night

It was soon time for school to start again. My last year! Steve was still working Friday and Saturday nights at Alpha Beta Produce Warehouse. He also cleaned horse stalls for some folk who lived not far from the Biola campus. I baby sat two little boys near the college each afternoon, cleaned their house and also worked a few hours a week at Sears in Buena Park. And we were both taking a full load of college classes. Needless to say, we were very busy.

For our Christian service assignment Steve and I were on a gospel team with two other students (another guy and gal). She played the accordion really well and they both enjoyed singing. We worked up some duets between my violin and her accordion and the four of us sang a quartet. Steve preached. Each Sunday night we went to a different small church in the area that had asked Biola for a team.

One of the churches that our gospel team went to was Calvary Baptist Church in La Puente. Steve and I both really enjoyed the church and the folk there. We started attending there on Sunday mornings. At the end of the semester our gospel team broke up and Steve and I began helping with the junior high group at the church in La Puente. We attended there every Sunday morning and evening. We made many good friends there (both young and old). It was so nice to have a home church that we enjoyed together. I played the piano at their services and we continued as leaders of the junior high group after we were married.

During that school year Steve sold the little Isetta and purchased a 1960 Rambler. We had it registered in my name (at my father's suggestion) since I drove the car almost as much as Steve did. That way we could insure it in my name and have it on Dad's policy. It was extremely expensive for a single young man to get insurance. (My Dad always knew how to save a few bucks). It worked out very well, except for one day when I got a notice from the Biola student court that I had a ticket for parking my vehicle at the men's dorm. So I had to appear at court and explain the whole deal. I was very relieved when they cancelled my ticket.

We had a very interesting Christmas that year. Steve had his night job at the produce warehouse and I was working for the Buena Park Sears store in the catalog department. Christmas was rush time at Sears so they offered me full time for the two weeks of vacation. Steve was also able to work full time. Since we were saving for our wedding and marriage we decided to stay at the dorms the two weeks of vacation.

I was the only one left in my dorm except for my dorm mother, Mrs. Carr, who had a little apartment in the dorm. Steve was the only one in the guys

April 1964, trying out our wedding arch used at our wedding reception.

dorm. Mrs. Carr had us over for supper a couple of times. It was so weirdly quiet and a little bit creepy being the only girl in that huge building. We were quite busy and did not see a lot of each other since I was working days and Steve working nights. We traded the car each morning and evening.

Christmas day Steve surprised me with a little pine tree that he had put in the back seat of the car and decorated. We put our few Christmas gifts under the little tree. Then we drove up to the mountains (actually found some snow) and opened our presents.

Times were different then. We could not find any place to eat on Christmas day. *Every* place was closed. We finally found a liquor store that was open and bought a frozen pizza. I baked it in the little kitchen in my dorm and we ate in the big empty lobby. Even Mrs. Carr was gone that evening. That was a very strange Christmas day.

FIVE

NEWLYWEDS

At last our wedding day arrived! (June 13, 1964)It was a gorgeous day. The church was full, and all went well.

We spent the first night of our honeymoon in a quaint little motel in Saratoga.

The next day we headed for Hume Lake, which is high in the Sierra mountains. We camped in a tent, did some hiking, swam in the lake, went

horseback riding and enjoyed just relaxing. The long two years of courtship and engagement were finally over. It was so much fun fixing our meals, hiking, swimming and being Mr. and Mrs. Steven King.

On our way back to Los Gatos we stopped at Tom and Susie's in Seaside. Tom was the youth pastor at the First Baptist Church of Seaside. They had a small apartment attached to the church building.

None of us will ever forget the meal that Susie and I fixed for our new husbands. Neither of us had ever done much cooking. We decided to fix a roast beef dinner with all of the fixings. We kept checking the cookbook for every dish. We even tackled an apple pie from scratch! The men wondered if they would ever get dinner. We waited a long time for the roast to get done and it was almost bedtime before the pie was finally baked.

Three months before we were married Steve and I had found a duplex home that had an empty apartment. The rent was only $65 a month. It was an older home about five miles from the college. It was on a little bit of land because there was a railroad track right behind the home. Land was very unusual in that area. We decided we better grab it , so Steve moved out of the dorm and into the house.

A very nice elderly couple, (Mr. and Mrs. Galbraith) lived in the other apartment. It was on a quiet street in an older neighborhood. We furnished it with odds and ends of furniture that were given to us from folk from our church. We bought an older stove and refrigerator from ads in the newspaper. After our honeymoon we brought a trailer load of furniture down that my folks had collected for us.

Steve told me that it was very quiet at night. Our first night in the house together I was awaken about 1:00 a.m. when the trains banged and clanged and changed cars.

The banging took place every night at that time only 30 feet from our bedroom window. Steve was so exhausted when he got home from work and hit the sack, that he had never heard the noise. It was a long time before I slept through all the clanging and banging. But we loved our little home!

We were praying that I would be able to find a good full time job to help Steve finish school. Our home was two blocks from the Buena Park Library. I had enjoyed working in a library a few summers before and had a good letter of recommendation from my former boss. So I walked down to the library, filled out an application and attached the recommendation. The next week I was called in for an interview and they hired me. What an answer to prayer! I could walk to work. We only had one car, so that had been a real concern.

It was a huge library. Besides books, one could check out phonograph records and even pictures for your walls. We did not have many pictures so we were able to have a different large picture hanging in our living room every couple of weeks. There was one western picture that I checked out quite often. And we enjoyed beautiful music from the library on our old phonograph.

The first few weeks I checked in books and put them on the shelves. I soon moved to the check out counter and after a few weeks was promoted to be the secretary for the assistant to the head librarian. That was really wonderful because then I had regular daytime hours from 8:00 to 5:00 Monday to Friday. The typing and short hand classes that I had taken at San Jose State the summer before had definitely helped me get the promotion. Of course, so had a lot of prayer. I was transferred to the day job before daylight savings ended so I never had to walk home in the dark.

One of my most vivid memories while living in our little home took place shortly after we moved in. Steve desperately needed a hair cut. (Back then he had hair). We decided that I needed to learn to cut it so we purchased a hair cutting kit. We asked Mr. Galbraith (our next door neighbor) if he could help. He said he had never cut hair before but that he had sheared a lot of sheep. So he came over to help. Steve had a sheared look for a few weeks and I became much braver at using the clippers. I never asked for help again.

It was really nice having the Galbraith's in the apartment next to us since Steve worked five nights a week (8:00 p.m. to 12:00 a.m.). It was like having our grandparents next door. I was very comfortable because they were there. Then due to sickness in their family back east, in January they had to move .

At that same time one of my former room mates from Biola, Jan, and her husband, Murray MacDougal had come to visit and were thrilled with our place. They were paying twice as much rent as us. They really liked our older neighborhood and especially the rent price. So they moved in when the Galbraith's moved out.

Living next to Murray and Jan was a real experience. They were both missionary kids. Jan had grown up in south Africa and Murray was from the Sudan in north Africa. They had each spent many years living in boarding schools for missionary kids and did not know a thing about keeping a house. They were also free from dormitory rules for the first time they could remember. They would knock on our door at midnight and want to go out for ice cream or pizza.

Steve still had his part time job working for a couple that had horses. (Along with carrying a full load of classes at Biola and working Friday and Saturday nights at Alpha Beta Produce warehouse.) He would clean the horses stalls, shoe their horses feet and exercise them in the round pen. (To Steve that was not work).

The couple had a little Shetland pony, Nugget, that they wanted to find a home for. She was in foal and they did not want to deal with two Shetland ponies. So Steve came home one day and said he had a pregnant pony for us. Well, I was rather shocked. "What will we do with a pony in the middle of Buena Park?" I exclaimed.

He convinced me that Nugget would get along just fine. He would build a little corral behind our garage. We did have quite a bit of room as the railroad was behind our home. There was not any homes between us and Buena Park Boulevard either and it was quite a ways from us. So there was a lot of space in our yard. What could I say when the landlady said it was fine with her? It did sound like a fun adventure.

Backing up a bit in time—during our first three years at Biola, one of the Physical Education professors, Dr. Fisher, kept a horse Adaph, (a beautiful registered Arabian stallion) on the campus and had a horsemanship class. Steve met him the first week he was at Biola and enrolled in the class. Steve and Dr. Fisher became close friends and Steve helped him with his horse. Steve would rake the corrals, feed the horse and was able to ride him whenever he wanted. Dr. Fisher had a trick riding saddle and taught Steve how to do tricks.

Steve had taken me (riding double) many times on Adaph when we were dating. The corrals were near the soccer field just below my dorm. We spent a lot of time at the horse corral.

Now (back to where we are in our story) Biola was concerned about having the horse and corrals on the campus because of liability. They could not justify the insurance necessary for a horse. Dr. Fisher sold Adaph and he needed to get rid of the corrals. Steve was sure the timing was perfect for us to take the Biola corral and put it in our backyard for Nugget. He asked our landlady and she said it would be just fine as long as we kept the manure raked up.

So we ended up with the Biola corral (most people think of the school choir when they hear those words) and Nugget in our backyard. Steve connected the corral to the garage and built a small lean-to shelter. A few weeks after Nugget came to live with us she presented us with a cute little foal. We named him Chipper. We ended up keeping Nugget and Chipper for many, many years. They lived with us for three moves and all three of our children learned to ride and drive with them. Nugget lived to be 40 years old.

One Saturday afternoon (before Nugget had her foal) Steve had tethered her out near the railroad track where she could eat some grass. Then he went to work. Fortunately I was outside, hanging laundry on the line when something spooked Nugget. She jerked her tether stake out of the ground and took off running right toward Buena Park Boulevard. It was a very busy four lane highway. I was running behind her, praying the whole way. Just before she reached the highway, a gentleman jerked his pickup truck off the road and into the grass. He jumped out of his pickup and grabbed Nugget's rope just as she was about to run onto the highway. He saw me running up the grass with tears in my eyes and handed me the rope. I gave him a hug and thanked him for being my answer to prayer. He just laughed, hopped back into his truck and took off as if nothing unusual had

Left: Peggy's college graduation photo, 1964. Right: Steve graduates from Biola, November 1966.

just happened. (Now who can ever say that God does not answer prayer!) We never tethered Nugget again in Buena Park.

Besides Nugget and Chipper, we had acquired a little kitten we named Smokey. Steve brought Smokey home one day shortly after we were married. She was a cute little gray kitten that had wandered into the yard of the folk he worked for. They didn't want him so Steve brought him home to me. I fixed him up with a litter box and he was so much company for me with Steve working nights.

The problem came a few days after Smokey arrived. All three of us were scratching. Oh how we were scratching! Smokey had fleas! Nothing that we bought over the counter helped. After many itchy days and Smokey being expelled from the house, we consulted a vet and found a powder that killed the fleas.

In the middle of all these activities Steve was still a full time student at Biola. One day during the annual Biola Missionary Conference, Steve was asked to drive to the airport and pick up one of the missionary speakers, Dr. David Clark. Dr. Clark was the Director of United Indian Missions. Steve had spent some time with UIM the summer before we were married when he was with Practical Missionary Training.

On the ride back to campus Dr. Clark asked Steve what he was interested in doing after graduation. When Steve mentioned that he was interested in Christian camping and missions, Dr. Clark told Steve about property that the United Indian Missions had just purchased south of Gallup, New Mexico for a camp. Steve and I had become very interested in Christian camping and were praying about finding a camp that we could work at when he graduated. That property sounded very interesting to us but we knew that we were going to have to work for at least a year following graduation to pay off college loans. We figured that by the time we paid off our bills they would have a director for the camp. So we did not think any more about it.

Just before Steve's graduation I put in my notice to resign at the library. I had enjoyed the job but I was really looking forward to Steve being the full time worker. We had made plans to move to Bend, Oregon for awhile where we would both work and pay off college bills. A few days after I turned in my resignation, my boss (who was the assistant librarian) and the head librarian for Buena Park Library took me out to lunch. We went to Knott's Berry Farm and had lunch with Mr. Walter Knott (the man who had started Knott's Berry Farm). It was a special treat to meet him. He was a very sweet elderly gentleman.

Thinking about our move to Bend, we sold the Rambler and purchased a used Dodge pickup truck. It had a push button transmission and was easy for me to drive. But it sure seemed big.

We were looking forward to leaving the congestion of southern California. We had made many wonderful memories during the four years we lived there attending Biola, but city life was not for us!

SIX

Life on a Sheep Ranch

Steve graduated from Biola on a Sunday afternoon. (And, yes, he wore his cowboy boots.)

My Dad and Mom had driven down for the graduation and helped us pack. At 5:00 o'clock the next morning we were in our truck, pulling a trailer with all our belongings and were headed for Bend, Oregon.

Steve had made sides for the back of the pickup so we could haul Nugget and Chipper back there. We pulled a U Haul trailer full of our furniture. Smokey rode up front in the cab with us.

We stopped at a campground along Shasta Lake that night and camped. Nugget and Chipper enjoyed getting out of the pickup for the night. And I was very relieved that they stayed tied all night. Poor Smokey! We were afraid to let him out.

The next day we made it to Bend.

We had made a trip to Bend during Steve's Easter vacation and visited with friends from his church, Bill and Noma James. Bill and Noma had a large ranch just south of Bend. Bill raised sheep and had many acres of hay. The Deschutes River ran right alongside their property. They had an old cabin just above the river that they said we could live in. For rent Steve would help Bill part time with the haying and with their horses and their sheep. It was a perfect set up for us. Bill was the Director of Civil Defense for Deschutes County.

We loved that little cabin even though it did not have running water or a bathroom. There was a little outhouse just behind our cabin. Our kitchen (which consisted of a stove, a refrigerator and a cabinet) was in a screened in porch. The cabin had one small bedroom and a small living room, which we heated with a little wood stove. We ate on a folding card table in the living room. I sometimes did the laundry outside in a wringer washer and more often did it at Steve's parents home in Bend. Steve's folks were very gracious with letting us come over for baths, which became a weekly Saturday night ritual. In between we used an old wash tub. It was great for me but a bit small for Steve.

If you were to go to Bend today, the ski resort, Inn of the Seventh Mountain is right across the Deschutes river from where our little cabin was.

We were active in the First Baptist Church in Bend. Steve had spent many years there. We helped with the youth group and enjoyed outings with the young married class. I sang in a trio with Suzanne (who had attended Biola with us) and with Ellen, who was dating Loren James (whose parents owned the ranch we were living on). We did a lot of singing that year at our church and traveled to other churches.

Steve and I enjoyed many fun times with Loren and Ellen. Since they were engaged and we were married, we were their chaperones on some neat trips. They both had good jobs and more money than us. One time we went to the Oregon coast with them for a weekend.

We learned a lot about sheep while living on that ranch . There was a big old ram named Buckles that roamed in our yard. Steve would try to drive him away with a shovel but most of the time the shovel would not even phase him. I was afraid of him. When I went to work each morning I always hoped that Buckles was not close as I dashed to the car.

We got to help shear the sheep. Many years later when Steve was pastor of a church, he realized how many sermon illustrations he gained from those months on a sheep ranch.

During August and September Steve spent his evenings in the hay fields helping the James family with the hay harvest. Mostly he raked the hay into furrows with the tractor and bucked the freshly baled hay onto the trailers by hand. He loved it. That ranching experience was also going to come in handy for him years later.

Shortly after we arrived in Bend we discovered that I was pregnant. We were really excited.

Steve had a full time job working for a produce warehouse. I got a job teaching kindergarten. I had about 15 students from 8:30 a.m. to noon each day.

I particularly remember one day when one of the little boys in my class got a nosebleed. After I had tried for several minutes (it seemed like hours) to get the blood to stop flowing, I frantically called Steve's mom. She told me to pinch it shut while applying ice and that she would be right over. By the time she arrived from clear across Bend the bleeding had stopped, but I was so relieved to see her. She stayed and helped me for the rest of the morning. I had her tell stories to the children about raising nine children. They were fascinated.

In July my folks came up to visit. My Dad spent his time figuring out how he could add to the cabin. He talked to Mr. James and they came up with a nice plan to double the size of the cabin (making a bathroom and kitchen and increasing the size of the living room.) Dad and Mom came back for a couple of weeks in the fall and started a nice addition to the cabin. By the time the snow came we had a bathroom in the house and a kitchen. The next year Loren and Ellen were married and moved into it. They made it into a lovely little home.

PART III

UNITED INDIAN MISSIONS BROKEN ARROW BIBLE RANCH

SEVEN

RAISING SUPPORT AND ANOTHER KING ARRIVES

Around Christmas time we received a very unusual letter from the United Indian Mission in Flagstaff, Arizona. It was a pink slip to a car that was registered to Steven King. It had the United Indian Mission address on it. We had no idea what it was all about since we had never been there. So Steve phoned the mission to ask about the car.

It turned out that the car belonged to a dentist named Steven King who had worked at the mission for a short time as a volunteer. He had fixed some of the missionaries' teeth. A young lady, Sandy, (who was temporarily acting as secretary at the mission) had attended Biola with us. She did not know of any other Steven King. So when the pink slip came to the mission headquarters she looked up Steve's address from mutual friends and sent it up to us.

While Steve had Sandy on the phone, he asked about the property that the mission had purchased for a camp. She said that it was still there and that no one had been chosen yet to go there. Steve said out of the blue, "Why don't you send us an application?" She did.

So because of a trip to the airport a year earlier to pick up Dr. Clark and a dentist named Steven King who fixed teeth for UIM missionaries and a temporary secretary who knew us, we ended up asking for an application for United Indian Missions.

By the time we received the application we were very excited about the possibility of becoming missionaries with UIM. We had paid off our bills with both of us working and living rent free in the little cabin.

The mission was having an orientation for prospective missionaries in March in Flagstaff. We were expecting the baby the first part of April. We decided we could go to the orientation and then get back up to my parents home in April and have the baby there. Mom and Dad were delighted. They had a bedroom, living room, and bathroom addition on their home that we could live in.

We stopped in Los Gatos and visited an obstetrician on our way to Flagstaff. My folks were so excited because we would be living with them when the baby was born. And they were very happy about our missionary plans. They kept our truck and loaned us their nice new car for the rest of the trip.

Steve's parents were very supportive but I know they felt sad to see us leave just before a new baby was to be born. We assured them that we would be back a lot when we were raising support. I was sure that the baby could be born in any hospital all along the way if necessary.

So we arrived at the United Indian Missions headquarters a month before our baby was due. We had a great time with all the staff that worked at the mission headquarters. Dr. David Clark and Allen Livingston, the Business Manager, gave us our orientation sessions each morning. In the afternoons we worked in the office and learned a lot of the workings of the mission. They had missionaries serving in the southwestern United States, in Mexico and in British Columbia.

I had trouble being of much help in the office because they kept telling me to go to our room and rest.

At the end of the session, we drove to southern California and were presented to the full board of the United Indian Missions at their Annual

Meeting (about fifteen men.). Two of our Biola College professors were on the Board. I remember that we shared our testimonies to the whole board. Then we were questioned individually. After that we both left the room while they discussed our applications, our testimonies, and our recommendations. Finally we were invited back into the room. The men all stood to their feet and welcomed us to the mission. They said we were now officially missionaries with the United Indian Missions.

After they all shook our hands and congratulated us, they recommended that we get in our car and head for Los Gatos. It looked to them like the two of us were going to become three at any moment. As we pulled out into the southern California traffic, we had such a peace. We knew that we were headed on a real adventure. We had a real goal. But it was also a bit frightening knowing that we now had to go out and raise our monthly support.

About that same time Steve received a draft notice in the mail. The country was in the middle of the Vietnam War and we did not know just what we should do. We talked to our pastor in Los Gatos (Pastor Blaine Bishop) and he told us that Steve had a special calling to be soldier for the King. He said that Uncle Sam recruited men and he would get his quota. The Lord depended on volunteers. So Steve answered the draft notice with news that he would soon be a parent. Fathers were not being drafted.

Steven Randall King, Jr. (Randy) was born on April 2, 1966 (two weeks after our orientation with the mission). Our obstetrician was Dr. Edmond. His father was the president of Wheaton College in Chicago. Dr. Edmond was a fine Christian man and because we were new missionaries just raising our support, he did not charge us for the delivery. That was such an answer to prayer. Randy was several years old when we finally finished paying the hospital bill with small monthly payments.

It was so nice to have that little apartment in my parents home. We spent our days writing and phoning every contact we knew for meetings. My Dad had many contacts with area churches that he wrote to about our work and our need for support.

While we were there my Aunt Nancy (who is a wonderful seamstress) made me several dresses that were quite cute and practical. I found after Randy was born that my clothes did not fit like they had before. I just expected to get right into them. I never did get back to a size 6.

Our Los Gatos church had a Missionary Conference when Randy was just two weeks old and we were their missionaries for the week. The main conference speaker was Dr. Warren Wiersbe. He was the pastor of the Moody Bible Church in Chicago, Illinois. It was so great and challenging to spend that first week of meetings with Dr. Wiersbe. Several times we went out to dinner or lunch with him. What a tremendous man of God he was. He had lots of good advice for us as young missionaries.

We had been given a Navajo cradle board while we were at the mission. headquarters. During the conference each evening we strapped Randy in the cradle board and stood next to a small Navajo hogan we had constructed for our mission display. We met folk and answered questions as best we could.

Randy (when he was a tiny baby) loved being in the cradle board. Later on the reservation we noticed the Navajo babies would be quite fussy but when their moms snuggled them secure in the cradle board they would nod right off to sleep. (IF their tummies were full and their bottoms dry).

Los Gatos took us on for $300 a month support. That was such a blessing and encouragement. Back then $300 was a good start toward our needed income.

Shortly after that conference we headed back to Bend for some meetings we had arranged in central Oregon. It was fun to go back to our little cabin for a few weeks. We spent several weeks there while Steve studied for his ordination. His pastor had arranged for quite a few Conservative Baptist pastors in Oregon to come and examine him for a recommendation for ordination. Since he had not attended seminary he knew that he would really be drilled.

Steve did a great job and was unanimously recommended for ordination. Now he was not only a father and a missionary candidate, he was Rev. Steven King.

Like Salt & Pepper

We received only one invitation for a meeting from all the many letters we had sent out to churches requesting meetings to present our mission. So we decided to go out and meet pastors. We bought a little homemade camper for the back of our truck. We three Kings lived in it on the road as we went looking for churches that would let us present our mission.

We found a lot of small Village Mission churches in southern Oregon. Steve would knock on the pastor's door and introduce himself. Very few pastors had ever heard of United Indian Missions but most knew of Biola College. We always left a pamphlet and gave some dates when we could be in their area. We began to get several invitations for meetings that way.

One day I remember in particular. We had driven into the little community of Idahna, Oregon. Idahna was located on one of the passes between Bend and Portland. It was pouring down rain and there was not a soul to be found around the little community church. Steve went into a store and asked how he could find the pastor of the church. The lady informed us that he was a school bus driver. Well, we had just seen a man under a school bus, working on the bus. So we went back and Steve stuck his head under the bus and introduced himself. Sure enough, it was the pastor. They chatted for awhile and finally he crawled out from under the bus.

"Any man who will stand in the pouring down rain for as long as you have, must have some kind of stamina!" He lined us up for a meeting. That little church in Idahna supported us faithfully the whole time we were with the mission.

Another time that Steve and I both vividly remember was when we were headed back to my folks place after a couple of months of meetings. We were flat broke. There was a man in Los Gatos who always hired Steve to work in his service station whenever we were back there between meetings. We were figuring to be in Los Gatos that evening so were not concerned about our lack of funds. But we had forgotten about the toll bridge in the Bay Area. When we saw the "Toll Bridge Ahead" sign we both thought, "Oh no! We don't have any money!"

I suddenly remembered that as a kid I used to pull the seats of the car up and look for money. Sometimes there was change under the seat. So we stopped at the side of the road and pushed our seat up. Sure enough we found enough change to get over the bridge. When we got to the bridge there was a sign that said, " Free Way." We did not have to pay the toll! Steve insisted that we stop and buy a coke.

During a meeting near Placerville, California a couple asked if we wanted a horse for the ranch in New Mexico. Of course, Steve immediately said that it would be wonderful. We were given Two Bits. Two Bits was an albino. He was white and had light blue eyes. His skin was very pink. I thought he looked rather sickly but he was Steve's first full size horse. Steve was so excited! Once again, I was wondering what in the world we were going to do with him. We already had Nugget and Chipper up in Oregon on the James ranch.

We had met some new wonderful friends, Royce and Marge Rickman, in Los Gatos. Royce was a pilot with United Airlines and they had a small ranch up in the mountains just outside of Los Gatos. Royce had already told Steve that he would help transport Nugget and Chipper to the ranch when we were ready to move. So Steve gave Royce a call and he told him that he would also keep Two Bits for us. Steve brought Nugget and Chipper down from Oregon to the Rickmans and Royce helped Steve go get Two Bits.

We spent a few months in southern California visiting and speaking in churches we knew from our Biola days. A good friend had a small cabin in a wooded area that he let us live in. It was wonderful.

Our church in La Puente took on some of our support. My cousin, Faith, and husband Dave were members of a church whose pastor was the son of Dr. Clark, the president of United Indian Missions. That church also took on some support.

A good friend from our church in La Puente suggested we contact her brother, Rudy Sautter, who was the pastor of a small church up in the San Bernardino mountains. So one day Steve left Randy and I in the little cabin we were staying in, and headed up the mountain to see if he could find Rudy. After winding around the mountain roads he finally found their home and knocked on the door. Three year old, Neil, answered the door and left Steve standing there as he ran to his Mom yelling, "Mommy there's a cowboy here!" That was the beginning of a long and lasting friendship with the Sautter family.

Steve had a very unusual experience the day that we spoke at Rudy's church. We presented our slides and mission presentation in their morning service. Then all the church folk went over to the Sautter's home for a pot luck.

It was pouring down rain and had been pouring for several days. The mountains were saturated with water. Randy needed some more baby formula so Steve left Randy and I at the Sautter's home and drove in the drenching rain to find a grocery store.

He was stopped by some men doing road work where rainwater and mud was rushing down the mountainside and across the road. While he was sitting there waiting, he saw a huge hunk of the mountain slide down and bury a man that was working at the side of the road. Steve jumped out of the car, ran to the spot, and yelled to the others that there was a man buried right there. They all started quickly digging with their hands (Steve still in his dress suit). Within minutes one man yelled, "I found hair!" They carefully dug around his head and he started choking and breathing. He was alive and the men soon had him unburied.

That little church took on some of our support.

Our full support was raised in a year. We were so thankful to finally be putting down roots.

EIGHT

Home at Summer Park Ranch

The acreage that UIM had purchased for the camp was called Summer Park Ranch. It was located in Vander Wagen, New Mexico.

The Rickmans were going to drive along with us to Vander Wagen in their truck and pull their horse trailer with Two Bits, Nugget and Chipper. A few days before leaving Los Gatos we found out that the horses had to have a physical exam and a certificate of good health to drive through Arizona. Steve and Royce had a vet out to check the horses. The vet discovered that Two Bits had a cold so he would not give the certificate. Royce said for us to go ahead. He and his family would come out with the horses when Two Bits was better. What great friends they were!

My Dad and Mom helped us drive our belongings to New Mexico. We had our truck and the mission truck. Randy really got tired of driving in that truck. He had spent his whole first year traveling and he hated it.

I'll never forget how happy we were to drive into Summer Park Ranch. It was Randy's first birthday, April 2, 1967. He had started walking at nine months old so when we released him from the car and showed him his new home he just ran excitedly from room to room. What a birthday present!

The ranch consisted of 40 acres of land (20 miles south of Gallup) purchased by the mission from Cena Gibbls, who was still living on the

Our home in Vander Wagon, 1967

property. Cena had sold the property to the mission very reasonably with permission to live on the property until her death. So the ranch consisted of her cabin, another cabin and our home. Our home had been Cena's for years but she had moved into a smaller place so we could have the bigger one.

The place was called Summer Park Ranch when Cena purchased the property and she let us know that she did not want us changing the name while she was alive. The camp is now named Broken Arrow Bible Ranch. The broken arrow is an Indian sign for peace, so what a great name for the camp.

Cena became a wonderful friend. She was a big Dutch lady and had been an army nurse for years. To some people she was quite intimidating but we loved her and she was so good to us. For many years she served as our camp nurse. She was so happy to be involved.

The ranch is dotted with pinon pines and ponderosas. The Navajos love the pinon nuts. The soil is very sandy with a lot of sandstone. The elevation is 6700 feet. It is not far from the Continental Divide.

Having been a carpenter for many years, my Dad was quite alarmed with the condition of our house. It had been built during the depression. The walls were just boards nailed to some studs with decaying old stucco on the outside. There was no insulation. Inside a lot of the wiring was visible. There was not any wall switches. The lights hung on cords from the ceiling. The lights turned on with a chain hanging from above the bulb. (Many a night, when we came in after dark, I wandered about with my hands in the air trying to find the bulb and chain. Steve would bump them with his head).

The bathroom consisted of the toilet, an old rusted tin shower stall and a little old sink that hung from the wall. A cracked mirror hung above the sink. There was not any cabinets in the bathroom.

The kitchen was built as a lean-to onto the home. At only 4'10" tall, I could stand up at the sink and touch the ceiling. I loved it. I could reach all the cupboards.

Steve and I (and Randy) were very happy to have a home. While we were dashing from room to room looking it over. My Dad was busy figuring out how he could bring a gang of men from the church in Los Gatos back to do some fixing up.

United Indian Missions previously had a children's home called Desert Jewels Home. They had closed the home because government regulations made it very difficult for the mission to operate. Most of the furniture left from the home was in our house. There was two big baby cribs, bunk beds, dining room furniture and living room furniture. It was great because we did not have much. There was even an old piano in the living room and it had a good touch. I was thrilled!

Dad and Mom helped us unload our belongings and get things settled. A couple of days later they took the train back to San Jose from Gallup.

The evening that Dad and Mom McKee left we wanted to call Steve's parents and let them know that we had arrived safely. Since we did not have a phone yet, Steve decided it would be fun for him to go down to Zuni and phone from there. We had never been there. Our new (to us) home was in Vander Wagen which is located on state highway 32 about 20 miles south of Gallup and 20 miles north of Zuni.

Zuni is a pueblo made up of old stone apartments. Steve wandered through the pueblo looking for a phone booth. Finally he asked someone where he could find a telephone. The man directed him to the police station which was in the pueblo. At the station there was a Zuni policeman doing exercises with barbells in the office with his few prisoners. He pointed to the phone on his desk and told Steve he was welcome to use it. The officer said that there was no public phone in the village. So amidst the confusion, Steve called his Dad and Mom and informed them we had safely arrived into a different world.

We got initiated into missionary life right away. The neighboring UIM missionaries, Howard and Louise Burns, were leaving on a deputation trip for a couple of months. We were going to help out at their mission while they were away. Their mission station was in an area known as Oakview which was about ten miles southwest of us. That ten miles was on a rutted gravel road.

Oakview consisted of the church, the Burns home, a trading post, the traders home and a government boarding school.

Howard showed Steve the trails he traveled each Sunday morning and Wednesday evening to pick up Navajos for church. They were sandy dirt trails that wound around and up and down out on the reservation just a few miles from our home.

The Burns left their pickup for us because it had a camper shell. We crammed close to fifteen people in the back of the truck and more up in the cab each time we had a service.

The day after the Burns left, a Navajo man came to our door. (It was our first introduction to Navajo ways). The man came in and sat down for awhile. He did not say anything. Just sat there. I gave him a cup of coffee and some cookies.

Finally he told us (in very broken English) that his Dad, Francisco, had just died and that we must help him. He said that we needed to go to the hospital and get the body and that we must build a box for him. And we were to have the funeral. Steve assured him that he would do what needed to be done.

As soon as the man left, Steve went to Cena's and called a neighboring missionary, Charles Girton, who lived about ten miles northeast of us. Steve had spent a week with the Girtons when he was with Practical Missionary Training three years earlier. Mr. Girton came right over and gave us some lessons on Navajo funerals. The man was right. The missionary was the undertaker and the funeral director.

The next day Steve and Mr. Girton took our truck to the hospital and picked up the body that was in a sack. They brought him back to our house and laid him on a tarp on the dirt floor in the garage. I instructed Randy that he could not go into the garage.

The next day Mr. Girton helped Steve build the box and they put the body in it. Some of the relatives had brought some clothes by. Jimmie, a Navajo man from the church, helped Steve put the clothes on him. Steve discovered that it is extremely difficult to dress a stiff, dead body. There was no way they could get the new cowboy boots on his feet. They finally just placed the boots the family had brought for him alongside the body.

If they could have put the boots on, it is tradition for the old time Navajos to put the shoes on the opposite feet. That way the spirits will be confused and will not be able to follow their tracks when they get to the hereafter.

After getting the body taken care of Steve went out to the man's home place where several Navajo men helped him dig the grave. It was good therapy. By the time they had dug for awhile everyone had relaxed and were telling fun stories about Francisco. Steve enjoyed getting acquainted with the men and learning more about Francisco.

Francisco was an elderly medicine man. He had many wives and numerous children and grandchildren. The church was packed for the funeral.

It was the first time we had ever experienced wailing. A lot of the women stood beside the box and wailed. It was really sad for those who did not have the hope for heaven. I took Randy outside because he was getting scared and started to cry. Steve gave a simple message of hope for those who know Christ. Some of the folk were Christians and many were not. You could definitely tell the difference between those that knew the Lord and those who did not.

The church had an old piano that someone had converted into an organ. They put an old vacuum cleaner motor in it. It would play really loud and then die out to almost nothing and then get really loud again. There was no way to control it. Playing for that funeral (and later several weddings and funerals) was very frustrating. I always cringed when I got called on to play that piano-organ instrument. It was all they had, so we made do.

NINE

LIFE IN VANDER WAGEN

Steve had a pleasant surprise when we first arrived at Summer Park Ranch. The 40 acres had an old wire fence around it. Cena had let a neighboring Navajo man, Tommy Nez, keep his horse, Flicka, and donkey, Charlie, on the property. There was not any corrals so Flicka and Charlie wandered the 40 acres. Two Bits, Nugget and Chipper were going to have company. Tommy and his wife, Dorothy, became good friends. They had a little boy, Danny, who was the same age as Randy.

Tommy and Dorothy were very happy to let us use Flicka and Charlie for camp in exchange for Steve training and feeding them.

One of our first days at the ranch we fixed pancakes for breakfast. (I say we because pancakes are always a joint project for Steve and I. I mix and he flips.) Charlie, the donkey, came to our kitchen door (that had a window in it) and knocked on the window with his nose. He loved pancakes and that became a ritual at our home. If we had pancakes, we had Charlie. He could smell them every time. He would come to the door, curl his lips back and beg with a big "Hee Haw". Then we would share a pancake or two with him. Our guests loved it.

We found out that Cena had been feeding him pancakes that way for months.

Going out our driveway to town to our car, which lived alongside Highway 32. Heidi is in Mommy's lap in the bucket, and Ruth is in the bucket, holding Randy. Steve and some extras share the seat and fenders. We drove ¼ mile this way to get to and from the car to our home.

When the Rickmans arrived with Two Bits, Nugget and Chipper, we turned them loose to roam with Charlie and Flicka.

After Burns arrived back from their deputation trip we started attending the Gallup Baptist Church on Sundays and Wednesday evenings. It was the church that Cena, our new friend from the ranch, attended. We made a lot of wonderful friends and felt at home there. It was so good to be settled.

Summer Park Ranch was located on what is called the checkerboard area of the Navajo Reservation. When the railroad wanted to put tracks through the southwest, the government divided up the land like a checkerboard. There would be a square mile of reservation and then a square mile of railroad land. After the railroad was built the railroad sold much of the land. So our area was a checkerboard of private land and reservation land.

White Water Trading Post in the town of Vander Wagon, 1969.

Most of the Navajos lived in hogans, which were round, constructed of logs and covered with mud or sod. Some constructed cabins that were covered with stucco with rolled roofing. They were called kins.

We could see a hogan from our yard that belonged to the Tom family. Cena introduced us to them right away. They had several children. The younger four loved coming over and playing with Randy. They were several years older than Randy. They enjoyed him and he loved them.

Sometimes they would come to our home after dark. We found that the Navajos often treated their children like little adults who were capable of making mature decisions. If the children did not want to go to town with them in the morning they could stay home. Then after dark when they got frightened they would wish that they had gone with Dad and Mom and come knock on our door. So we would let them sleep in sleeping bags on our living room floor and send them home the next morning. Cena had started that routine when she lived in our home.

We soon became acquainted with many of our Navajo neighbors. None of them had water at their hogans. They came to our pump house (which was in our front yard) from miles around to fill their water barrels. Most had three or four barrels in the back of their pickups. They paid us 50 cents a barrel to help with the pump bill. So all day every day we had Navajos coming for water.

Right next to the well house and water faucet, Steve built a sand box for Randy. He had some nice tonka trucks and some buckets and shovels. They began to disappear, so we found another spot for the sandbox (a long way from the water faucet). That solved the problem.

Steve enjoyed getting acquainted with our neighbors by riding up to their camps on Two Bits or Flicka. The men loved their animals and it was a common ground for a visit. Most families had a group of two or three hogans or kins close together. A kin was a small rectangular shaped home. As a member of the family married another hogan or kin was built. Usuallly the young couple built on the land of the bride's family. The group of homes was called a camp

Most of our Navajo neighbors had small herds of sheep. They just let them roam. When they wanted to eat one or sell a few, they went out searching for them.

We learned very soon that time did not mean anything to the Navajos.

Shortly after we moved to the ranch, I was asked to play the piano at a Navajo wedding (down at Oakview on the instrument that I just hated). The wedding was scheduled for 2:00 o'clock in the afternoon so I arrived there about 1:45 p.m. Just as I got there the bride and some of her friends were piling into a pick up and heading for Gallup.

I ran over to the Burns home and exclaimed, " It's time for the wedding. I just saw the bride and her attendants leave. What's up!"

Louise started laughing at my surprise and explained, "The bride just decided that she wanted flowers for the wedding. They just took off for Gallup. It will take them at least a couple of hours." Oakview was about 30 miles from Gallup and none of them seemed the least bit disturbed about the time.

A few months later we attended a Navajo rodeo in Gallup. The clown was dressed up like a white man and was all wrapped up in a chain with a big clock attached to it. He kept stumbling and falling because of the clock. Obviously they thought we were just as crazy as we thought them to be about this time thing.

TEN

MEAGER BEGIINNINGS

Our main assignment was to start a camping program at Summer Park Ranch. We decided to start by having a day camp that first summer (1967). Two teenage boys came out to help us—Steve's 16-year-old brother, Paul, and Denny Smith, a 16-year-old from my brother Tom's youth group.

The campers came from Ft. Definance Arizona and from Oak view (the two area United Indian Mission churches). Guy and Reva Kinney and Ruth Douglas were the missionaries at Ft. Defiance. Ruth came out and helped at all of our camps. Guy, Reva and Ruth were such an encouragement to us.

The campers enjoyed a sling shot range, games with Nugget, Chipper and Charlie, relay races and other games. We served a lunch out our kitchen window. Steve (with the help of Denny and Paul) had built a lean-to shelter onto our garage to eat under. In the southwest thunderstorms are frequent so the shelter was very necessary. The campers also enjoyed Bible stories and songs in our living room.

That first summer one of the games we played each day was the Trash Hunt. A lot of trash had collected on the property over the years so we divided the kids into teams and gave a prize each day to the team that collected the most trash. It worked great. By the end of the week we had a huge pile of trash to take to the dump and the property looked much better. Fortunately the mission had an old dump truck on the ranch.

After the camp was over Steve and Denny and Paul constructed an open shelter out of logs they cut and peeled. Steve put a corrugated metal roof on it. The shelter was a real help for the following years of camp. It was located away from our home and out near where we were planning to put the main camp building.

We discovered that first summer how violent the New Mexico summer thunderstorms could be. Very frequently a storm would blow in and light up the skies. They usually consisted of torrential rains, gorgeous lightning and roaring thunder. One such storm came while Steve, Denny and Paul were nailing metal roofing onto the shelter.

Steve told the boys they could tell how far away the storm was by counting "a thousand one, a thousand two, a thousand three", etc., after each lightning bolt. Then when you heard the thunder you could tell how many miles away the storm was by which number you were on. So they tried it after the next lightning bolt. They all leaped off the roof when a LOUD thunder clap came immediately after yelling "a thousand one!"

That fall we had two other teenage boys, Ron and David, come live with us. Both boys had been struggling in school and were concerning their parents with their choice of friends. Ron was from my home church and David was from our church in La Puente. They stayed with us for a couple of months.

Steve, Ron and David started digging the foundation for the basement rooms of the dining hall and kitchen building we were planning to construct. I think by the time Ron and David had dug almost everyday for the two months, they were quite ready to go back to school and behave themselves. They were really nice boys, got along well together and were a big help.

While we were on deputation to raise our support we had spent a weekend at a youth camp in Oregon. We were really impressed with the multi-purpose building that they had. Steve spent a lot of time at the retreat copying their plan.

One afternoon, shortly after we moved to the ranch, Dave Clark- the Director of UIM, Don Fredericks—the US Field Director and Guy Kinney—our area director, all came out to discuss future plans. They were wonderful men of God and so encouraging. Steve showed the men the plans he had for the multipurpose building that contained the kitchen , the dining hall, restrooms and office building. He showed them the location he thought would be a good for the multipurpose building and for cabins. They liked the plans and gave him full approval to move ahead.

Steve sent rough sketches of the plans to an architect friend we had in Los Gatos. He made the blueprints for the large multi-purpose building. Since Carl was an architect in California the building is built strong. Downstairs there are bathrooms with showers, several bedrooms and storage rooms. Upstairs there is the kitchen, two offices, a small bathroom and the large dining hall. Now all we had to do was raise the money and build it.

That winter turned out to be one of record snow and cold. The road into the ranch turned into a thick gooey mud that became impossible to drive in. We left our truck out by the highway and went by tractor to and from the house to the highway. We were quite a scene going out the road on that tractor. Steve drove with almost two year old Randy on his lap. I (very pregnant) was perched on the fender. Usually we had Cena and her sister-in-law Grannie Garnett (who was living with her) riding in the front bucket of the tractor. That was how we went in and out to town. We did not go very often so when we did the ladies liked to ride along. We would leave our car out by the highway.

One day I realized that all of my shoes were in the truck . Each time we went out I would put on my boots and change into my shoes at the truck. Then on the way back I would put my boots back on and leave the shoes in the truck.

Grannie and Cena loved it when Steve would lift them high up in the bucket. They were really characters and we enjoyed them both. They were in their 80's and were each hard of hearing, so always had to shout at one another.

Steve said that listening to Cena and Grannie reminded him of three elderly ladies who were riding on a train together. The first one looked out of the window and declared, "It sure is windy today." Which made the second exclaim, "Oh no, Dear. It's not Wednesday it's Thursday." Then the third answered, "Yes, I'm thirsty too. Let's all go get a drink." Grannie was the mother of Esther VanderWagen (who was the wife of the trader at our trading post, Ernie VanderWagen). Cena was Esther's aunt.

Our area was called VanderWagen. It was named after Grandpa VanderWagen, a pioneer missionary in the area with the Christian Reformed Mission. Vander Wagen consisted of the trading post which was less than a quarter of a mile down the highway from the SPR entrance gate.

The trading post was a large old sprawling stucco building that contained a small store, the post office, and the trader's home. We had a post office box there and could buy milk, bread and a few groceries. It was very expensive and limited so most of the time we shopped in Gallup

The trading post was a place where the Navajos could trade for their groceries or money. Ernie had a safe room that was full of rifles, Navajo jewelry and rugs that had been traded. When the Navajos needed money or supplies they could trade for it. Later when they had enough money they would buy their goods back. He was very fair with the people and they all really liked him. (Sadly, a few years ago while driving his car, Ernie was hit head on by a drunk driver and killed.)

Ernie and Esther became great friends of ours. They had four children, Bertha, Janice, Joyce and Little Ernie. They taught us a lot about Navajo customs and ways. They attended our church in Gallup and their youngest kids (Joyce and Little Ernie) came to camp.

Grannie and Cena often came over in the evening for a game of scrabble. They were so much fun. They each had lots of interesting tales to share of there lives. None of us had a television set, so our evenings were spent reading, talking and playing games.

Steve was busy making plans for our first summer of overnight camps.

We had the shelter built for meetings and had built some out houses for restrooms. And we had collected a variety of tents.

We had written in our letters to supporters that we could use tents. We were sent a real assortment from our supporting churches and friends. The fun part was that most of them were old and did not come with directions. Each time we received a tent, we had a real puzzle. We would lay the pieces out in the yard and guess how it went together. Some were simple and some were a real challenge. Some were large and some were small. Some were in great shape and some left a lot to be desired. But we were so thankful for them.

Our home had a covered and screened back porch off the side of our kitchen. It contained a trap door that opened to stairs that went to a partial basement. The basement was wonderful for storing food for camp, as there was not any extra storage space in my tiny kitchen. The only trouble was that the door was very heavy.

One time I was in a hurry to get something from down in the basement and did not secure the door well. I made it almost to the bottom step when the door came crashing right down on my head. It actually knocked me out for a few minutes. When I came to I realized I was sitting on the floor of the basement in the dark. (Now I realized what people meant when they say they were seeing stars). I was able to push the door back open. Aside from a bump on my head and a headache, I was just fine. I was so glad that I did not have Randy with me. Oftentimes I carried him when I went down. I learned a real lesson about that door. And Steve made a hook so that we could secure it.

ELEVEN

ANOTHER SON and the UNEXPECTED DIAGNOSIS

We were expecting another baby and were so excited. Randy and the new baby would be 22 months apart.

There was a Christian clinic and hospital just east of Gallup in Rehoboth, New Mexico. The town was named for the Rehoboth Christian Reformed Mission. Rehoboth Mission had the hospital, a church and a boarding school. Most of the missionaries went to Rehoboth hospital as they had some really nice doctors and they were open to the public.

It was a Saturday, February 17 1968. The next few days we will never forget.

I was two weeks overdo and felt enormous. My little suitcase was packed and plans were made to drop Randy off at the Girtons home, on our way to the hospital. The pains started about 2:00 on a Saturday afternoon. We delivered Randy to Charles and Iris and then arrived at the hospital about 5:00 p.m.

My doctor was away on a skiing trip so the only doctor on duty was an extern (a student doctor who is not even an intern yet). He asked a few questions, checked me over and told us he thought it would be awhile so maybe we would like to go get something to eat. I really did not feel like eating so I got checked in. Less than an hour later the pains were quite severe and really close together. Steve called the nurse and when she checked me she exclaimed, "My goodness the baby is coming!." When the extern delivered Rusty (Russell Lance) at 6:20 p.m. he said, "I am sure glad you did not go out to dinner." So was I!

My doctor, Dr. John Kamps, returned on Monday morning. He came in to see me accompanied by a nurse. By the looks on their faces, I suspected that something was wrong. Dr. Kamps informed me that he was very concerned about Rusty. He had a lot of characteristics of a Mongoloid (in 1968 the name Downs Syndrome was not used.).

For some reason my immediate thought was, "Well, we can handle this". Their news was a shock but I had a real peace. Of course, I was extremely anxious to see Steve and share this together with him.

Shortly after Dr. Kamp's visit, Dr. Al Diddams came into see me. He was a young surgeon who went to our church and was soon to become our very best friend. It just so happened that when Steve had returned from the hospital on Saturday (just after Rusty was born), there was a note on our door at the ranch from Al. It said , "Steve, I just bought a pony can you help me with it?" Well, that was the beginning of a long friendship and a partnership in several horses with Al.

Al had just heard about Rusty and had come to my room to ask if he could help with the diagnosis. He had a very good friend who was a pediatric specialist and was temporarily up at the big PHS Indian Hospital in Gallup. He was from South America and was only going to be in Gallup for a few weeks. If we agreed, he was sure that he could get him to come take a look at Rusty. I was naturally quite thrilled for the help. Al and Dr. Kamps were friends so we knew that he would be happy for his help.

Steve had no idea about any of this yet. When Steve came in to visit me that evening, he passed the nursery and saw the 3 doctors (Al, Dr. Kamps and the specialist) all standing around Russ's little crib. They were tossing him into the air and catching him to see his reactions and were obviously having quite a discussion.

"What are Al and Dr. Kamps doing with Rusty?," was his comment when he came into my room. I can still see the concerned but loving look on his face when I explained their suspicions. And I'll always remember his comment. "I wonder why God would pick us for this?"

We were saddened but we both felt like if this was so, then it was the will of God for us and there was a purpose. No one else in either of our families had this type of problem. We both had a real peace.

The three doctors soon returned to my room to inform us that Rusty was a puzzle. He had excellent muscle coordination and was physically in good shape, but they were still quite concerned. He had so many physical characteristics of a mongoloid. They suggested that in a few weeks we take him to Albuquerque for blood tests. They explained that people with mongolism have an abnormality on the 21st chromosome that would show up in the blood.

We took him home and began to think that it was all a big mistake. Rusty was so healthy and so good. He very seldom fussed and he ate well.

When Rusty was a month old our good friends, Royce and Marge Rickman and their three children came to visit us. Royce was a pilot with United Airlines and they had flown to Gallup from their home in Los Gatos, California in Royce's private airplane.

We told them Rusty's story and mentioned that the doctors wanted us to take him to Albuquerque for blood tests. Royce said that he would be happy to fly us there in his plane. Well, that sounded like a real adventure. Neither Steve or I had ever flown in a small airplane. That would make the hard trip fun.

We left Randy with Royce and Marge's three teenagers at our home and took off in the small plane from Gallup to Albuquerque. It was a beautiful day but the air currents in the southwest can be really something. I remember I was sitting in the back seat next to Marge holding Rusty on my lap. He was strapped in an infant seat. All of a sudden the airplane dropped down and the infant seat was above the level of my head! I grabbed it and pulled him back down. Marge and I still laugh over that.

Steve almost fainted, I cried and Rusty screamed when they took a lot of blood samples. But it was all over very quickly and we had a great flight back to Gallup. Then we had the long wait to hear the results.

About 3 weeks later Al (Dr. Diddams) drove the twenty miles all the way out to our house to tell us that nothing unusual showed up in the blood tests. Rusty was a normal boy!

TWELVE

First Summer of Overnight Camps and the Blessing and Encouragement of Friends

About a year later Al told Steve that he was very interested in getting some horses. We already had their pony, Cinnamon, out on the ranch. His kids and Randy enjoyed riding our three ponies and Cinnamon almost every Sunday afternoon. Al asked Steve what type of horses he thought would be good to raise. Steve had always been interested in Morgans, so he suggested that they look into them.

Shortly after that Al came out to the ranch with lots of books and information on Morgan horses. It was not long before Al and Steve made a journey to Albuquerque to visit some Morgan ranches. Al purchased a beautiful Morgan mare that was bred. He also purchased a huge truck load of hay for all the horses. We had been buying hay for our horses almost every week and bringing it home in our station wagon. We were thrilled to see a whole load of hay. And no more constantly trying to vacuum hay from the floors and seats of our car. (Now that there was four in the family we no longer fit in the cab of the truck. We had sold our pick up and were given a nice used station wagon from our church in Los Gatos).

We were able to obtain a lot of empty wooden ammunition boxes for free from Ft. Wingate, which is just a few miles east of Gallup. A youth group from a church in Albuquerque helped us construct a barn with them. Steve made a tack room in it and used the rest of the barn for hay storage. He attached some log corrals next to the barn.

Another youth group had helped us build an arena for horse and pony games out of logs we got from our area. During camps we used the arena for a lot of games with the ponies and Charlie. Nugget, Chipper and Charlie were camp favorites. Two Bits was also a real nice calm horse for our camp staff to ride. Steve and the counselors enjoyed riding Flicka also.

Two weeks after Rusty was born, my Dad arrived with two men who were going to remodel our bathroom. One was John Matthies who was a tile layer. He brought a metal tub that he had constructed for our bathroom. They tore out the old metal shower and put the tub in, lined it with tile and made it a bathtub- shower combination. It was wonderful.

Before John made it to our bathroom he had to walk through our kitchen. His first comment was that he wanted to come back next year and tear out our rusted metal drain board and bring some tile out for it. The other men agreed and began to make plans for new cabinets. They did a great job with our bathroom. It was just in time for the busy summer ahead. And John did come out the next year with a gang of men who put new cabinets and a lovely tile drain board in our kitchen.

This year (1968—our second summer on the ranch) we had the shelter built on to our home for the campers to eat under. We had the tents for cabins with an outhouse in each tent area. And we had built the log shelter for meetings.

My brother, Tom, was now the youth pastor of our home church in Los Gatos. He had a large youth group and was training a select group of teenagers for counselors for camp. These kids met with him every Tuesday morning before school. He had classes on everything from leading a soul to Christ to learning how to have a servant attitude and work hard.

Most of these teens came from very wealthy families so living in a tent on the ground with our Indian youth was a culture shock. Often times I would have a counselor come to the house to store some of her belongings (i.e. extra clothes, cameras, curling irons and makeup). I remember one gal coming and saying, "Peggy, I am so embarrassed to have all this stuff. My girls only have a paper sack containing just one or two changes of clothes."

We ran three weeks of overnight camps that summer. One for 4th through 6th grade boys and one for 4th to 6th grade girls. The last week was teen camp for guys and girls. Campers came each week from Window Rock and Ft. Definace area, the Havasupai and Hualapai reservations and a few from Zuni and Albuquerque. Larry McClannahn, a Navajo from Window Rock spoke at our teen camps and Gary and Ruth Hasenauer spoke at our two junior camps. Ruth Douglas was our camp dean for all of the camps. Several campers made decisions to accept Christ at each camp.

My Mom came out with the bus load of counselors and helped with Randy and Rusty while I cooked. She was such a help.

There were two small homes on the ranch besides ours. One Cena lived in. The other we used to house our girl staff during boys camps and the boys staff during the girls camps. It worked very well.

So the counselors that were in the tents for the week came to our home to wash up and shower. Sometimes as many as 15 of us were sharing our one little bathroom. Someone truthfully made the comment, "We never give the seat time to cool!" We were very motivated to have the bathroom and shower section of the new building finished for the next summer.

After eating the campers got in line with their dirty dishes. We set up a garbage can for scraping—then three wash tubs on a table for rinsing, washing and finally a disinfectant rinse. Each camper washed their own dish and silverware. We had a staff person at the end to check for cleanliness and then the camper dried their dish and silverware and stacked it. We had a cup rack with the campers names, where each camper hung their cup. They could come to the cup rack for a drink of water throughout the day.

The tents worked for our camp cabins but some of them were a real challenge. We had one tent we named "Gone with the Wind." It was a big wall tent and it held a lot of campers. But every time a big wind came along it blew down. Summers in the southwest are blessed with fantastic electrical storms and gorgeous sunsets. The electrical storms are usually accompanied by drenching rains and strong winds. We have many memories of leaking tents.

I remember one counselor, Rolane, coming to me and asking if I would please pray for her tent to stay up that night. Yes, she was staying in "Gone with the Wind." She said, "I don't think I can jump up one more night- hold up the tent and tell the girls that we sure are having fun as we prop it back up again." We prayed that the tent would stand and that she would be able to handle it if it didn't. The tent did stand.

Many ladies from our supporting churches had donated handmade quilts that we loaned to the campers who came without bedding. That happened a lot. Every weekend we would air the quilts out in the sun and after all the camps were over I would haul them all to Gallup and launder them at a Laundromat.

The Girtons daughter, Estelle, helped us out by playing the piano at our services and was one of our counselors. She was a student at Multnomah Bible School and was an excellent piano player. For camp we had moved the piano from our home out to the open shelter. (The shelter had a log wall on the front side of the building where we had a platform for the piano and a podium for the speaker.) Once at the beginning of an evening service, Estelle sat down to play the piano and it would not play. When the top was opened to investigate, a huge gopher snake was discovered curled up in the piano. Estelle almost fainted on the spot.

One of our campers, Steve, Dr. Diddams son, caught the snake. He put him in a crate, named him "Ralph", and stored him in our garage right next to my freezer. Steve would come in quite regularly (with some of his camp friends) to play with him and feed him. I was very relieved when that camp was over and Steve took Ralph home. I think Sheila and Al took him back to the woods somewhere and turned him loose.

While we were living with my folks in Los Gatos and raising our support, we became friends with Dick and Betty Oliver. Dick was a block layer and did gorgeous rock work. He had told us if we ever needed any brick work done he would help us.

The fireplace in our home was in a state of disrepair. We could even see daylight through some of the cracks.

So Dick and Betty also came out that summer. They brought their family and their camp trailer. While Dick fixed the fireplace, Betty helped me in the kitchen. They had two teenagers who helped with the camp program.

It was the middle of camp when Dick had the fireplace torn out, so for a few days we would run in and out of the big hole in the living room wall. Someone said, "I think you have literally burst at the seams!"

Steve and Dick had an interesting experience when they went to Zuni to get rock for the fireplace. Steve had been told that Zuni was the place to go to get beautiful rock slabs. So he had talked to the Zuni Indian man who had been recommended to him for the purchase. He told Steve that he had plenty of rock and to just bring Dick out and they could pick it up.

When they finally found the man (it took a while) in the pueblo of Zuni, he jumped in his pickup and told them to follow him. They left the pueblo and ended up in a rock quarry several miles out of Zuni. He said to Dick, "What do you want? We'll break it off of the cliffs for you." So that's what they did for several hours. He chunked out beautiful rocks. Dick (who was a stone mason from San Jose, California and built several fireplaces a day on big housing developments) was flabbergasted. He was thrilled with picking out his own rock and getting to really design it right from the quarry. But he was not used to the time that it took. The fireplace turned our beautiful.

Dick and Betty have several children. Their youngest, Darlene, has Downs Syndrome. Darlene was about six years old that first time they came to visit. I shared Rusty's story with Betty and told her that the blood tests had proved Rusty normal. Later Betty told me that her heart ached for me because she knew right away that Rusty had Downs, no matter what the tests had said. Rusty was so much like Darlene had been at the same age. We had a lot of long talks. Although she never told me her conclusion, she let me know that if Rusty did have Downs Syndrome, I was greatly blessed.

Also that summer, one of our counselors was Mindy Fox. Mindy's father, Tom Fox, was the son of Dale Evans. (Tom was a teenager when Dale married Roy Rogers). He had a little sister, Robin, born to Roy and Dale. Robin had Downs Syndrome and died when she was very young with the mumps.

Tom and his wife Barbara came by the ranch to pick up Mindy when the camps were over. They were on their way to visit relatives in Texas. They were pulling a camp trailer and stayed with us for a couple days. We had a wonderful time with Tom and Barbara and it was the beginning of a lasting friendship with them.

We shared about Rusty. Tom told his mother, Dale Evans. She wrote me a nice letter and sent an autographed copy of her book, "Angel Unaware". It was the story of Roy and Dale's little Robin who had Downs Syndrome. That was so thoughtful and such an encouragement to us. She even called once on the phone to see how Rusty and I were doing.

In the coming months I just could not believe how different my two sons were. I had always thought of Randy as being an easy going happy kid. But Rusty was something else again. When he woke up from his nap, he would just sit and play. He never demanded to be held. He had no interest in getting up and walking. He was a year and a half old and still content to pull himself along the floor like a little hop toad.

But when there was a lot of excitement or he was over tired, he screamed nonstop and would not settle down. Al prescribed a sedative that worked great. We carried it everywhere with us just in case it was needed.

I remember a few times at church noticing Al staring at Rusty with that "concerned doctor's look" about him. I thought that he also was having lingering doubts about him.

A pediatrician (Dr. Stam) moved to Rehoboth about the same time I became pregnant again . Al suggested we make an appointment for him to see Rusty. Dr. Stam was a big kind young man with a very gentle way about him. He examined Rusty for a long time. Then he quietly told us that he did not care what the test results said, he was certain that Russ had Downs Syndrome. We later learned that some people with Downs Syndrome do not have it in all of their blood cells. It is called mosaic as some cells are normal and some cells are not. So maybe that was why the blood test was normal. Or maybe there was just a mistake in the testing.

He explained that the term Mongoloid was no longer used. A doctor with the last name Downs had done a lot of study on the disorder and so the name Downs Syndrome was the new term.

By now we were not the least bit surprised with his diagnosis. I can say that we have never felt bad for ourselves because of the diagnosis, but we often feel bad for Russ when he can not keep up with others his age.

THIRTEEN

She's the Girl Type

There was a lot of snow that year. As quickly as Rusty came, we were anxious to get me to the hospital the minute I started having pains. The doctor was also concerned and admitted me to the hospital. Just after I was admitted all the labor stopped. But knowing our past experience and since we lived so far out and the snow was so deep, they kept me in the hospital. Finally, a day and a half later, January 27, 1970, Heidi Joy was born, weighing in at a big 5 lbs. 2 oz. She was tiny but all was well!

While I was in the hospital Steve was busy remodeling our front room. The room had old stucco that was falling off. So he had a friend come over and they tore the whole ceiling off. They put up a new ceiling and lined the walls with a nice knotty pine siding. Our dining room, which was right next to the living room, had a big closet with a top shelf. Steve put 4 year old Randy up on the shelf so he could lay up there and watch the men work. He put Rusty in the play pen. The boys had a great time but they were both covered with sheetrock dust. Actually the whole house was covered with sheetrock dust.

Dr. Diddams and his wife, Sheila, had stopped by to see Steve. Sheila could not get over the sheet rock dust everywhere. Between my doctor having heard of the condition of our house, Heidi being so small (she had lost

a few ounces so was just under five pounds) and the temperature in Gallup dropping to 30 below zero, I had to stay in the hospital some extra days.
I was sure a happy camper when they finally let us go home. Fortunately, since Rehoboth was a mission hospital and we were missionaries there was not any charge for my long hospital stay.

Heidi was so tiny. I put her in a bassinet right by our bed at night so that I could hear her breathing. She thrived well and did great!

Once again that summer(1970) we ran three weeks of camp. One for teens, and one for junior age boys and one for junior age girls.

That fall Steve went on a deputation trip by himself to Pennsylvania. We had two churches from there that supported us. We had never been in their churches so we felt we should make this contact.

Calvary church in Los Gatos had recently given us a ford station wagon. The church had a club for high school boys interested in mechanics. Folk would donate cars to the club. The boys (and the mechanic who helped with club) fixed them up for missionaries.

Steve drove the station wagon and brought his tent, sleeping bag, camp stove, and ice chest along to make the trip more reasonable. It was in November. The southern states were warm enough to be sleeping in his tent but when he got up into the northeast he really had to bundle up at night. He had some good meetings and thoroughly enjoyed the folk back there.

He was really excited because he was able to meet his Dad's brother, Uncle Lloyd, who lived in West Virginia. All his life he had heard his father speak of him but he had never met him or his family. They were thrilled to meet him also. They simply could not believe he had been sleeping in a tent. He spent a night and several hours the next day with them.

Meanwhile back at the ranch in Vander Wagen (while Steve was gone on the trip), it was my birthday and I was having one of those "I'll never forget the day" experiences. It was just after lunch. Heidi was sleeping and Randy was playing. I put Rusty in his little walker and decided to grab the moment to wash my hair. While my head was in the sink I heard a loud scream from Rusty. With my head all sudsy I ran to find him. I found him alongside the little electric heater in his bedroom. His poor little leg was terribly burned. He had pushed the bedroom door open to find his toy box and hit the heater with his leg.

I quickly gave him three baby aspirin (I just guessed that is probably the most I should give an almost two year old) and tried to calm him. He was tired and I was able to pat him to sleep. I could see that the burn was really bad. It had taken off a lot of the skin.

I knew I needed to get Rusty to a doctor. But I did not look forward to taking a baby, a four year old and an injured two year old the eighteen miles to Gallup by myself in our old truck. Joan Kenn, a UIM missionary, was now living in the little cabin next to Cena's. Cena was away that day. I knew that Joan should be home soon from teaching a release time class. So I decided I would have her rush me in to Gallup to see Al as soon as she got back. I called Al's office and he said that he would wait for me. Finally, I got the suds out of my hair, got it set and covered up.

When Joan returned we rushed to Gallup. Al said that the burn was deep but that he was sure Rusty would be fine. He applied some medication, wrapped it. Then he instructed me to bathe him in a warm bath, let the dressing fall off in the tub and then redress it with the medication he gave me for the next few days

That night when Steve called from back east to wish me a happy birthday, I burst into tears and told him the whole story. I had been so brave until I heard Steve's voice.

After our phone conversation, Steve called Al (Dr. Diddams). Al told him not to worry. He would take good care of his family while Steve was away. The next evening before I had a chance to change Rusty's dressing in the tub, there was Al at my door. He changed the dressing and showed me just what to do each day to keep it clean. How many folk have a doctor like that? We were 18 miles from Gallup!

Rusty healed quickly, but as it healed the burn formed a large keloid scar on his leg. It covered quite a bit of his little leg.

Two years later when Rusty was about four years old the keloid scar (which was located a couple of inches above his knee down to an inch

Our family, left to right: Randy, Peggy, Heidi, Steve, and Rusty, 1970

or two below his knee) was drawing the skin together. Steve and I really did not think anything about it. We thought he was doing fine. So I was surprised when I walked into the church nursery one morning and found three doctors, Dr. Diddams, Dr. Buker (a surgeon friend from the big PHS Indian hospital) and Dr. Schmidt (a young plastic surgeon who was doing his residency at the Indian hospital) all looking at Rusty's leg. (He had short pants on that day). They were examining his scar. They told me that they were concerned that the huge scar was drawing his skin together at the knee and that it should be removed..

I went and got Steve. Gearhart (Dr. Schmidt) told us that he would be glad to remove the scar with some plastic surgery. Al said that he would assist so they could do it at Rehoboth Hospital. Gearhart laughingly told us that he could not charge us since he was with PHS. So with our overwhelming approval they set up a date to operate on Rusty.

The surgery went really well. Steve actually got up enough nerve to watch it. (I sure did not). They took a razor blade and pealed off the scar. Then (also with a razor blade) they pealed off a piece of skin from his other thigh and taped it over the wound. After taping the piece of skin on the wound, they wrapped it well with an ace bandage. The skin would attach itself and cover the wound. Amazing!

We took him home the next day. A couple of days later (after Rusty's nap) I went in to see how he was doing. I was shocked to see him sitting in his crib in the midst of the bandage. He had unrolled all of the bandage and was just about to pull the tape and new skin off of his leg. He was undoing the whole surgery!

Immediately I rewrapped it and called Al. Al said he should have known better and put a cast over it. So once again we rushed Rusty into Al's office and he put a cast on the leg to protect the skin graft. (Rusty was getting to be quite a favorite with Al's staff). The graft took and now he just has a small scar from where they took the skin for the graft and a scar where the burn was.

We just could not get over how this all came about from the church nursery. God was certainly taking care of us. Some of us mothers jokingly said we might attract some new visitors to our church if we announced a well baby clinic in the nursery.

Broken Arrow Bible Ranch, multi-purpose building (above) and Steve building at S.P.R., 1971 (right).

FOURTEEN

FRIENDS, BUILDING AND BILLY

We had some good Navajo friends (we'll call them Joe and Sarah) who had a little girl the same age as Heidi. They came over one day and asked if they could move into the little cabin that we had built for the camp. We used it for staff to stay in during camps and planned on moving it to our cabin site when we had our multi-purpose building completed. It was a simple 12 x 20 foot cabin with an outhouse behind it.

Joe and Sarah (like many Navajos when they first get married) were living with Sarah's mother and her big family. Sarah's mother "ruled the roost" and Joe was getting tired of it. He was ready to leave Sarah if he had to continue living with his mother-in-law. Well, Steve decided they could stay there for a few weeks, IF Joe would start building his own hogan up on their place. Joe said he would. So they moved in.

Well it wasn't long until the little cabin was really looking bad. They were settling in and it was obvious that Joe was not building a hogan. So Steve said, "Joe I am going with you, out to your place, every morning this week and we are going to get that hogan built. I have to have this cabin in a couple of months for camp."

Steve had the most interesting experience working with Joe and other family members—cutting the pinon pines for the hogan, limbing them and then actually building the octagon house. Then they put mud in the cracks and put rolled roofing on the roof. They laughed and joked together and it was a great time. In less than two weeks they had a nice hogan built. And we helped get Joe and Sarah and their baby moved into it.

The funny part of the story happened just a few years later when we went by Joe's place. The hogan was gone! Now that Joe and Sarah had a few more kids they had moved back in with Grandma. We stopped by to chat and Steve asked what happened to the hogan. They just shrugged and said that they needed firewood that winter, so they needed to burn the wood from the hogan. Now they were perfectly content to be living with Grandma again.

Often we went to a Navajo celebration at one of the neighboring missions or a community event. They usually served Navajo fry bread with pinto beans or mutton stew. When cooking for camp I often had one of the teen age Navajo girls or a neighbor Navajo lady come help me make fry bread. Fry bread and beans or stew is still a real favorite in our home.

Steve was once asked to marry a young couple and was privileged to experience a very traditional Navajo wedding celebration. After the wedding they invited just a few folk into their hogan for a special feast (fire roasted goat's head). Steve said you could see the goat's skull and it still had a little of the hair scorched on it. It was very interesting but not something he ever relished eating again. He said that he just made sure he was eating something solid.

Back in our camp story, Steve and John Chariton (our missions maintenance man) were making big headway on the bathrooms. The bathrooms were the first part of the new building. We were going to have flush toilets and showers for our next summer of camps! There was four toilets and four showers in each bathroom. We would still be cooking in our home and serving the meals out our kitchen window.

Drilling for water was interesting. We did not realize how far one had to dig to find a trickle of water in the arid southwest. The well driller finally found some water at over 600 feet. We purchased a huge storage tank for water and later another tank was added for even more storage. We limited the campers' showers by not having any hot water (just lukewarm) going to the bathrooms.

John came every Monday morning to help with the building. He spent the week days with us in our home. Randy and Rusty called him Grandpa John. He took a little nap on our living room rug each afternoon just after lunch. While he was sleeping Randy loved to hide his hat. When he woke up they played a "find the hat" game. Later in the spring he brought his camp trailer out along with his wife, Millie. The kids called her Millie Mom. We all loved Grandpa John and Millie Mom.

Ruth Douglas was helping us a lot. She spent all her summers with us, so it was decided that she should move her mobile home on to the ranch property and live there. During the winters she was busy with release time classes in the area boarding schools. It was really fun having Ruth next to us. Cena and Granny enjoyed her, too. She was a Cherokee Indian and had a wonderful way with the campers. Her great sense of humor kept us laughing.

Ruth Douglas and some girls at camp.

Ruth sometimes walked and talked in her sleep. One morning (when John Chariton was staying with us) Ruth came over and exclaimed, "I woke myself up last night shooting my gun. I was standing outside the trailer with my gun in my hand!"

The guys went over to her house and saw a hole in her trailer but could not find the bullet anywhere. They told her that it was definitely not safe for her to have a loaded gun in her house so she took the bullets out of it. One day, months later, Ruth came over laughing. She was working on her slide presentation for a speaking engagement and found the bullet lodged in the middle of her slides. We all got a good laugh over that.

Steve had to take water out to the corrals in barrels he had in the back of our pickup. Then he would siphon the water from the truck into the horses' barrels. That was just taking more time than he felt he should be spending on animals. Down at Oakview Mission we had become acquainted with a boy named Billy. He had dropped out of school even though he was only 11 years old. He kept running away from the boarding school so his mom just let him stay home. The Burns suggested that he could probably be a help to us and we could really help him.

So Billy would come and water the horses for us. Oftentimes he would spend the night. His visits became longer and longer. He never seemed to want to go home. And when we did take him home he was knocking on our door the next day with his suitcase. His Mom liked having him stay with us. She said we were good for him. So we built him a little room on our back porch and put a bunk bed in it.

Billy became a part of our family. Shortly after he moved in we took him to Albuquerque with us to do some shopping. We went up an escalator in a store in their big mall and heard the funniest sound coming out of Billy. It was Billy's giggle. Then we realized that it was his first time on an escalator. They did not have such things in Gallup. So then we had to go use the elevator and show him what that was like. It was really fun to go up and down the escalator and the elevator with him. We rode each several times. Much cheaper than Disneyland!

The next year we took Billy with us on a trip to visit some of our supporting churches in Oregon and California. He was sure we were at the ocean when we reached the Columbia River. He had never seen so much water. (Our area of New Mexico does not have any streams—let alone rivers.) It was cute. He giggled and giggled when we crossed the Columbia River on the big bridge. Later on the trip we took him to see the ocean. He was so fascinated how the water kept coming and going on the beach. He said, "It just keeps coming back."

About that same time a man from Gallup (Bert Cottington) came to visit us at the ranch. He said that he had a Morgan stallion that he was hoping he could board at the ranch. He had heard we had Morgans. Since Al had a nice Morgan mare, the stallion sounded great. So Profilio was added to our growing herd. Being a stallion he had a separate extra strong corral.

One morning shortly after we got Profilio, Steve came in from feeding the horses quite confused. "Nugget and Profilio both have their tails chopped off!" he exclaimed. (Something strange was going on).

Steve mentioned it to Ernie Vanderwagen when he went to pick up our mail. Ernie laughed and said he was sure that one of our neighbors, who was a medicine man, had chopped them off. The Navajo fertility ceremony that is held for girls requires the tails of a young mare and a young stallion. Since our horses were corralled and the Navajos let their horses roam, we had the perfect set up for his needs. This was to happen to us several times while we lived there. The tails always grew back.

By the fifth summer (1971) we had the large camp kitchen built on top of the bathrooms (with plans for a large dining hall attached to the kitchen building) The building was situated on a slight hill so that the entrance to the dining room could have a large deck at ground level and bedrooms would be constructed under the dining hall and near the bathrooms. There was a big empty room downstairs alongside the bathrooms that would be for storage.

Another big project we had been working on was the cabins. Several work crews from supporting churches had come out and helped us build cabins out on the far side of our play field. They were simple rectangular cabins with five bunks in each cabin. They would hold nine campers and the counselor.

We had a circle of cabins for the girls and another circle group for the guys They were each located in a nice grove of pinon pines. They did not have to be set up and they did not leak or blow over. What a great addition the cabins were! No more leaking tents!

We had also been able to purchase a large swing set. It was placed over near the cabin area.

We had also moved an old small building (that we were able to get for free for moving it) on to the grounds. We made the front into a guest room (because it had a little bathroom). The back we used for a craft house. The campers could come during their free time and work on handcrafts.

Millie Chariton helped me with the cooking that summer. We had to cart all the meals from the upstairs kitchen to the downstairs of the building, We got our exercise and were extra thankful for our energetic teenage helpers. Millie was a lot of fun to work with.

We had been given a big commercial cook stove. It had eight burners and two ovens. John had built beautiful cabinets with a lot of counter space. He also made a large center cabinet with a chopping block on top. He spent many, many hours building that chopping block and since then many hours have been spent preparing food on it.

We also had obtained a commercial dishwasher. Our camp staff rotated each week between counseling and being on clean up tasks. The large kitchen was so great after cooking in our tiny little kitchen in our home the two years prior.

There was two offices just behind the kitchen. One was Steve's office and the other was nice for the camp records and office machines. There was also a small bathroom upstairs between the kitchen and the offices for the cooks and office workers.

The first part of the building with all the plumbing (the kitchen and bathrooms) was constructed. The largest part was yet to build (the dining hall with dorm rooms downstairs for speakers and guests).

Like Salt & Pepper

We had put a really nice redwood siding on the outside walls of the building. The Calvary Church in Los Gatos had helped us with purchasing it. We were going to need a lot more of the siding for the new addition. My dad had found us a good deal on the redwood in San Jose and the church was going to help purchase it again. We just had to go to San Jose and get it.

So a few weeks after camp was over Steve arranged to pick up the mission truck in Flagstaff and then go on up to Los Gatos and load up the lumber. Well, the rest of us (Billy, Randy, Rusty, Heidi and I) all wanted to go along. We tried to figure how we could all fit in the truck. It had stake sides, so I convinced Steve that he could have one year old Heidi and three year old Rusty up front with him and Billy and Randy and I could ride in the back of the truck. Billy and Randy and I promised we would not be a problem. So he agreed to take us all along.

We traded our van for the truck in Flagstaff. Billy and I sat on blankets with our backs up against the cab in the back of the flatbed. The three kids were up with Steve until dark. Then we moved Randy back with Billy and I (where we all climbed into sleeping bags and put a tarp over us). Heidi and Rusty fell asleep up front.

We were not too far into the Mojave Dessert when a California highway patrolman stopped Steve. I had seen the red lights coming and quickly pulled the tarp up over the three of us in the back. I told Billy and Randy, "Be real still, don't move or say a word."

The highway patrolman talked for a long time with Steve. California had a rule that all trucks like that one needed a commercial license to drive through California. The truck was registered in Arizona where a commercial license was not necessary. So he was informing Steve that he would have to stop in Barstow at a DMV and purchase a license for permission to drive the truck in California. All this time the three of us in the back were not moving, hoping he would not look under the tarp. (It was years before seat belt laws so we were not illegal). I just did not want to be seen lying there under the tarp.

Well, we were soon on our way again and the three of us in the back could wiggle and giggle again.

Back row, left to right, then clockwise: Steve, Grandpa McKee, Grandma McKee, Billy, Randy, Heidi, and Rusty, Christmas 1972.

We had a nice visit with Mom and Dad and a lot of other good friends. Then the real fun came on the way back from Los Gatos when the truck was loaded with the lumber. Steve and Dad, built two strong cubicles (like telephone booths) on each side of the front of the truck bed (one for Billy and one for me) before they loaded the lumber. At each stop we climbed up the side of the truck and then down into our little spots. It was really funny. (There are some times when being small comes in handy.) I would scream over to Billy every once in awhile to see how he was doing. Steve had a lot of story and song cassette tapes for our three little ones up front. Well, we finally made it home with the lumber and had made more fun memories.

Now we had the huge dining hall addition to build and God once again answered our prayers for help. A building contractor from Phoenix, Bud Ford, had contacted the mission and asked if there was a construction project that the mission needed help with. Bud and his father, Ira (who was a retired builder), came out and stayed with us for several months. We had Bud, Ira, John, and Steve working on the building full time. Bud was used to getting buildings constructed right and as quick as possible. Billy was a good help. He was their runner (retrieving this and that for them). Randy was in school/

I enjoyed cooking and hosting them. They were really fun. Our little house was very full at meal times. Bud and Ira slept in one of the office rooms behind the new kitchen..

By camp time, 1972, we had the dining hall under cover. It was so wonderful not to have to cart the food downstairs. We used the downstairs rooms for staff housing and for the snack shop.

We were so thankful for all that had been accomplished in those first four years.

That summer we had seven weeks of camp. Campers included Navajos, Anglos, Hualapais, Havasupais, Hispanics, and Zunis. The seven weeks started with a week of staff training, The last week was a retreat for United Indian Missions missionaries.

Sarah Garrison, a dear lady from our La Puente church, came out to help cook. Sarah scared me to death when she had just arrived. She walked into the kitchen and immediately passed out. After laying her down for a few minutes she was fine. At our high elevation we had that happen more than once.

We always had someone come live in our home for the summer to help with our kids. Then I could get up early to help with breakfast without waking up Randy, Rusty and Heidi. Two summers we had a really sweet widow lady stay in our home. Her name was Mrs. White and the kids loved her. Then we had a sweet girl named Sue. Sue would put Rusty and Heidi up on Charlie (the donkey) and take them all over the place in the mornings.

Dick and Betty Oliver came out again that fall for several weeks. Dick built a massive rock fireplace in the dining hall. Once again Steve and Dick went to Zuni and cut the rocks out of the rock quarry.

Shortly after the fireplace was finished a good friend from our church, Dr. Gerry Buker, (another doctor who worked at the PHS Indian hospital) told us he had a huge ox yoke that he thought would be just right for the big fireplace.

Gerry had found the ox yoke back east. It was so big and unusual that he had to buy a ticket for it and put it upright next to the seat beside him in the airplane. We hung the ox yoke on the fireplace with the Scripture verse "Take My yoke upon you and learn of Me."

Royce and Marge Rickman came out to visit again and brought Randy an appaloosa mare we named Polka Dotty. She was a nice little filly. Randy really loved her. We called her Polkie. She was added to the camp corrals and used for camp.

FIFTEEN

COUNSELLOR TRIP TO SUPAI CANYON

We liked to take our camp staff on outings. It was fun to get to know them better and it was a fun way to thank them for all their help. Often times we did this on a weekend in the middle of camps or just after camp was over.

One year we took the gang to Havasupai Canyon after all the camps were over. Supai is a tributary of the Grand Canyon and home to the Havasupai Indian Tribe. United Indian Missions has a mission station down there. They always sent kids to camp and had asked us to speak at their church sometime.

Tom and Susie drove down from Los Gatos and met us at Peach Springs (since most of the gang we had with us were from their youth group). We brought six year old Randy with us and left Rusty and Heidi at home with Mrs. White.

The trip to Supai is extra exciting for a bunch of city kids. We took old route 66 from Gallup, through Peach Springs, Arizona and then turned off the pavement onto a graveled road. We pumped along on a on it for about 60 miles where it ends at Hilltop. Hilltop is a big dirt parking lot. There we parked our vehicles, unloaded our gear and horses. We had brought a couple of our horses along to carry our gear and food.

Counselor trip to Havasupai Falls.

    It did not take Steve long, with the help of the guys, to get the horses loaded. We each had a pack on our back with our own personal stuff.
    The narrow trail switch backed down the side of a deep canyon. After we reached the bottom, we hiked for several hours. It was about 100 degrees and shade trees on the trail are nonexistent. So when we reached the stream near the village, we took off our shoes and waded and splashed. Some of us just sat in the stream. It felt so good!
    The Havasupai village is in a beautiful wooded area.
    There is a nice campground down there near four gorgeous waterfalls. Since it is so remote (and only reached by the long hot hike) there are very few campers. We were the only ones there that week. The campground is maintained by the Havasupai tribe but is a part of the Grand Canyon National Park. We set up camp and just relaxed. The gang enjoyed seeing the falls. One has to climb through a small cave to get to the last waterfall.

It was great fun swimming and hiking with the young people. There was one big drawback. Mosquitoes! Randy looked like he had the chickenpox by the time we left three nights later. If a mosquito is in the area, they find him. He must have sweet blood!

We had decided to leave for home after the church service (which was an evening service). Remembering the hot trip hiking in, we thought leaving in the evening would be much more comfortable.

When we reached the bottom of Hilltop (after the eight mile trek from the village) it was just after midnight and we were all exhausted. We definitely did not want to climb the steep switchbacks up the canyon until morning. So we found a nice spot off of the trail, stretched out in our sleeping bags and immediately fell asleep.

My sleeping bag was between Steve and Susie. About 3:00 a.m. I started feeling rain drops on my face. The men were both sound asleep but Susie and I woke up and began talking about what we should do. When we had fallen asleep the stars were bright and there was not a sign of rain. We had kids and gear strewn all over the place. Suddenly we heard a loud crack of thunder and the heavens opened. It began to pour. Everyone awoke and we all ran for the rock cliff next to us. There was a lot of small crevices in the side of the cliff. We each crawled into a crevice, curled up and tried to go back to sleep.

Steve made sure that the horses were secure. We told the gang we were making memories! We sure were.

By dawn the rain had stopped. We crept out of our holes in the rocks and assayed our situation. All our sleeping bags and gear were soaked. We decided to throw the drenched sleeping bags over the horses and a couple of the guys led them up to hilltop. They had to make several trips. The rest of us organized the remaining gear, put it on our backs, and started the trek up the steep canyon switchback trail to the vans (most of us in squishy wet shoes).

After fixing a breakfast of hot tomato soup and/or cold cereal and rolls (and other leftovers), they headed back to California and we headed back to the ranch. We had made more memories!

SIXTEEN

LIFE AT THE RANCH and a MEMORABLE FAMILY TRIP

The Sautter family (whom we had met on deputation from the mountains of southern California,) came to visit us a couple of years after we had moved to SPR. They really fell in love with the camp and the country. Rudy was a lay pastor and a school teacher. The Sautters felt led to sell their home in California and move out to help us at the camp. Rudy got a job teaching in Gallup and they put a mobile home on the ranch.

They were a great help. Carolyn was an excellent help in the kitchen and their two teenage daughters, Kathy and Becky, were great counselors and excellent with the horses. Annette and Neil, their youngest, were fun to have around. Randy really enjoyed Neil, who was two years older than him.

Rudy tutored Billy with school work. Eventually, when Billy was high school age, we were able to send Billy to a Christian Indian boarding school in Phoenix for a year. His favorite part of the school was getting to play on the basketball team. He only wanted to go one year.

Our lives fell into a regular pattern of camps during the summer. Most winters we spent several months traveling on deputation, raising money for the building projects. The fall and spring months were spent on construction, recruiting staff and making plans for the next summer's camping season. We spent a lot of time hosting guests and helpers.

We made many wonderful memories during our winter deputation trips. That was when we visited our supporting friends and churches and shared a slide presentation of what was happening at the camp and in our family.

The first few years we had a pickup truck with a camper shell. We had a boot between the cab of the truck and the camper bed. Steve built a frame for a mattress right behind the boot so that the kids and I could climb from the front of the truck to the bed in the back. Under the bed we had a box full of toys. He had put a carpet on a board that fit on the floor of the truck. So it was a great arrangement for traveling with kids. We had great times playing in the back of the truck. Once in a while I would drive and Steve would stretch out and sleep for an hour or two. We fixed picnic meals.

When Randy was 8, Rusty was 6 and Heidi was 4 we decided to take a family vacation. A trip with no meetings! It was the first of September, just after camp was over. We had purchased a pickup truck with a camper. We traveled in our camper through the Rocky Mountain National Park in Colorado and up to Yellowstone National Park.

When we entered Yellowstone we were given a little pamphlet which showed all of the hiking trails The first day we visited Old Faithful and some of the usual sights.

The next day we decided to take a hike into the back country. We saw a trail that was just a few miles from our campground that looked like it would be a nice hike (the Cache Creek Trail). So early the next morning we drove our camper to the trailhead and started out. We hiked and we hiked and we hiked. According to the pamphlet it looked like surely we would be coming to the end of the trail soon. The trail ended back at the highway and looked like it was just a few miles down from the trailhead where we had left the camper. We had brought along some boxes of cracker jack and some fruit, which we ate around noon.

Like Salt & Pepper

After our snack we finally met some other hikers (who seemed quite surprised to see a young family way out where we were). We showed them our map and they said that we were probably closer to the highway by continuing on rather than turning around. We had climbed almost to the top of Saddleback Mountain. They did warn us that we were going to have to cross the Lamar River. They said that we would be able to cross it with the kids.

After a lot more hiking, the trail became very vague and it was getting dark. Thankfully the trail was marked on trees with trail markers. Sometimes I would sit on the trail with the kids while Steve went ahead and looked for the next trail marker. Then he would yell from the marker and we would creep ahead to find him. By this time Steve was carrying Rusty piggyback and I was sort of dragging Heidi behind me by having her hang on to my back pockets.

We started to see signs of bears. Our little pamphlet told us that if we saw bears we were to roll up our windows and not open our doors. (Now that was a lot of help). We got really close to a huge moose.

At about 10 p.m. we came to the Lamar River. Steve found that he could walk across it. The water at its deepest was just above his waist. So I sat on the one side with Heidi and Rusty while he carried Randy piggy back across. He left Randy with instructions not to move and quickly came back for Heidi. He then crossed the river again and left Heidi in Randy's arms and came back for Rusty and I. I hung on to his back pockets (because the river was swift) while he carried Rusty across. Finally we were all across the river. Steve and I were sopping wet. Not long after that we saw car lights from the highway. What a relief! When we finally reached the highway we had to hike a ways on the road to our campground.

At the campground the three kids and I all collapsed in Randy's little tent. Poor Steve! He had to get back to the trailhead for our truck and camper. Fortunately, there were some campers still sitting up playing a card game. (It was almost 1:00 a.m.). Steve told them our story and they graciously drove him back to where our camper was.

The teepee we stayed in at Glacier National Park.

The next morning Steve met a park ranger and showed him where we had hiked. The ranger was shocked and told Steve we had hiked almost 20 miles. That did not surprise us at all. Steve suggested that they put some mileage indicators on their pamphlets or on some of their trail markers.

We were all tired and sore (but so grateful that we had not met those bears). Just outside of the park there was a place called Newberry Hot Springs. It had a huge swimming pool filled with the hot springs water. We stopped and all soaked in the pool for several hours. It really made our sore muscles feel good. While visiting with folks at the swimming pool someone mentioned how far away it was to Canada. Steve and I really laughed when Heidi piped up with, "We hiked to there yesterday!"

After our swim we headed farther north to visit our good friends, Jerry and Tiann Buker. They had been in our church in Gallup. Jerry had been a surgeon at the PHS Indian Hospital in Gallup and he had brought us the big ox yoke for the fireplace that was in the dining hall. Now he had a private practice in Montana. They wanted to take us to Glacier National Park to camp for a few days.

Jerry had gone to Glacier the day before and set up a large Indian teepee out in the forest (miles from where any body else was camped). He had put buffalo hides in it. So we were able to eat and play on buffalo skins in a real teepee with a fire in the middle.

After our first night, Jerry and Steve left early to go fishing. Tiann and I were sitting outside the teepee watching the kids play. Jerry and Tiann had three young daughters. A ranger came by and seemed surprised to see us way out there. He was posting BEWARE signs on trees saying that a large grizzly had been seen the day before in the area we were in. We gathered the kids, went back into the teepee, kept the fire burning and sure were glad when the guys returned. We had sung all the songs and played all the games that we could think of with the kids. And we had burned up most of the wood. It was quite chilly high up in the Glacier mountains in early September

That is a vacation that we will never forget. We made so many wonderful memories. We had seen parts of Yellowstone and Glacier that most people do not see.

SEVENTEEN

Full Home Full Life and Camp Growth

A couple of years after Billy moved in with us a Navajo lady, Bessie, came to our door and asked if her son, Darrel, could live with us each week from Monday to Friday and go to school on the school bus. Most of the Navajo children lived in boarding schools during the school week because it was impossible for school buses to go out on the reservation roads. Darrel was very shy and kept running away from the boarding school. She was so worried (and rightfully so) that he would get hurt. He was ten years old. Since he was a cousin to Billy and we had a bunk bed in the room we had built for Billy, we said, "Sure." Randy was in school by then and enjoyed having Darrel sit with him on the bus.

So each Sunday afternoon Bessie would drop Darrel off and then would pick him

Darrel, age 11.

back up on Friday afternoon. Billy and Darrel got along great and our kids loved them. With five kids in our house, there was never a dull moment. We did not have a television set so games and puzzles were popular in the evenings. Cena and Ruth loved to come over and play games with us and we all loved having them come.

We also bought a leather craft set and enjoyed making things with the guys. The Navajos are excellent craftsman and Billy and Darrel were very good with the leatherwork. Steve and Billy and Darrel each made themselves a nice pair of moccasins.

Dorothy

I have a beautiful Navajo rug and a silver with turquoise and coral necklace that Bessie gave me for keeping Darrel.

The next year a Navajo couple that often attended our church in Gallup asked if their daughter, Dorothy, could stay with us and ride the school bus into high school. Dorothy was a beautiful, sweet girl and was a senior in high school. They had moved farther out onto the reservation and did not want Dorothy in the boarding school. So we put Dorothy in Heidi's room. She was wonderful with Heidi. Heidi was two years old and cried if I left her with anyone but Dorothy.

We really enjoyed our full house. We purchased an old ford van and had a lot fun outings with our houseful. On Friday evenings we often went to Gallup High School Basketball games.

We had never ever had any inspections on our camp buildings. Steve had inquired with the county and the state when we first started construction on the buildings about building permits. He was told that if we owned the property (which the mission did), we could just build. That was really unheard of for most of our builders who came out to help us from California.

So it was a real surprise to us one spring day when a man drove up and said that he was the area health inspector and asked to see our camp kitchen. After a thorough investigation of the kitchen he decided that all was well except that we needed a big hood over the stove. He said that we could not have a camp without the hood because of fire danger.

We did some checking and found a Christian man from Window Rock who could construct one out of sheet metal for about $750. We did not have $750 so asked all our friends and the mission to pray.

We had a most interesting answer to that prayer.

Don Fredericks, the Director of United Indian Missions, was speaking at a church in the Midwest and mentioned our need. A farmer had decided to sell a tractor that had been sitting in his field unused for several years. He sold it to a young couple for $750. Then he told them that he did not want the money. He wanted the couple to give the $750 they were paying for the tractor to someone in need. Well, they had just heard Don Fredericks tell his church about our need for $750 for the hood. They quickly called up the church and told them to contact Don and tell him that they had the $750 to donate for the hood.

The next year the couple that had purchased the tractor came out to visit us and see where their money had gone. We had a wonderful visit with them. They stayed for a week and helped on a few projects.

With all the company we had and all our volunteer help, we decided it would be good to have an additional home on the ranch. We had saved some money so we purchased a small three bedroom mobile home, set it up on the ranch and moved into it. Billy slept in our camper. Dorothy and Darrel had both moved back home with their folks.

Cena was so excited. She was able to move back into her home. And it was fun for us to have the new home. That left the home Cena had been in available for short term help.

Heidi's kindergarten teacher, Patty, lived in the home for a year.

After a few weeks of kindergarten I noticed that Heidi was scratching and scratching her head. A good look at her scalp and I discovered her poor little head had lice. I was horrified. Washing her hair every night with the awful smelling special shampoo (that was suppose to kill the lice) did not seem to work for long. They kept returning.

One day I stopped into Heidi's classroom and noticed the children playing. They had several play stations. One station was where the students played house. It included hats and wigs that the children put on. It suddenly dawned on me that I might have discovered the problem and suggested to Patty that she try getting rid of the hats and wigs. She agreed and the problem was solved.

After Patty moved into town, John and Mindy Peterson came for a year to help and stayed in the home that Cena had been living in. Mindy had helped us as a camp counselor a few years before she married John They were interested in missions and wanted to help for a short time missions project. John's parents were missionaries to Japan, so missions was not new to John. They later became missionaries with Youth with a Mission.

We had a milk cow for our personal use for several years. John and Steve enjoyed many theological discussions while milking the cow.

One cow experience I will never forget. Steve was training a colt so he had put the colt in the horse trailer while he milked the cow. The colt kicked one of his back hoofs out of the top of the back door of the trailer. While Steve was struggling to put the hoof back in, the colt kicked Steve in the eye leaving a huge bloody gash. Steve tied his handkerchief around his head and continued to milk the cow.

When he came in to the house, I took one look at him and decided we needed to rush him to the clinic and get some stitches. So we did. It was at least an hour after the kick that we arrived at the clinic. Then we sat and waited for his turn. By the time the doctor saw him his face was so swollen it took a whole spool of thread to stitch it together.

Well, the next week, Heidi was riding Nugget in the arena. Nugget jumped at something and Heidi went flying off, hit the fence, and slashed her eyebrow open.

Steve grabbed Heidi, came running into me and said he had to rush to the clinic with her. When he arrived the nurse could not believe it. She could not believe he was the same man. This time he was a nervous wreck. It was his little girl. So they stitched up Heidi and removed Steve's stitches.

After John and Mindy's visit was over good friends Mark and Lorraine DuBois moved into the cabin. They were friends from Gallup Baptist and were fun to have on the ranch.

About that time I got really sick. I felt so tired that I could not even walk from the kitchen to our bedroom and I could not keep anything in my stomach. I had very seldom ever been sick and am one who makes myself get up and function even when I am not feeling well. I very seldom missed a day of school when I was a kid and had never missed a day of work. I'm afraid I did not have much sympathy for sick people. I thought they ought to get out of bed, get going and then they would feel better. Well, not this time. Steve knew there was something definitely wrong so he called Al (Dr. Diddams).

Al had him bring me in to his office. One look at me and he thought a blood test would show I had hepatitis. He was right. I was horrified to find out that the only remedy for hepatitis is complete bed rest. He said I had to promise to stay in bed at home or he would put me in the hospital. Fortunately he was able to give shots to the rest of the family so they would not catch it.

How thankful I was for my wonderful husband. He became "chief cook and bottle washer" and took care of seven year old Randy, five year old, Rusty, and three year old, Heidi. The folk from Gallup Baptist often sent meals. And the ladies at the ranch were great. Four weeks of bed rest did the trick. The last few weeks I learned I could do a lot from my bed (i.e. type thank you letters to all our supporters and fold the clothes). I read Rusty and Heidi lots of books and did a lot of coloring with them. It sure gave me a better appreciation for folk that are sick. I know that I am now much more sympathetic to folk who are ailing than I had been . (I sure wish I did not have to learn some things the hard way).

The most exciting occasion that happened about then, was the dedication of our big multipurpose building. It was finally finished!

We had a big banquet in the new dining hall and a really nice service of dedication and celebration. Many folk who had helped on the building were able to attend. The bedrooms downstairs were filled with overnight guests. Both Dad and Mom McKee and Dad and Mom King were able to come out.

About this same time Ellis and Grace Honaker came on our staff full time. Ellis was a retired pastor and a very excellent handy man. He had come out and helped Steve lay the flooring in the dining hall. After that visit they decided to join us full time.

Ellis was a wonderful help in so many ways. Grace was a great help in the kitchen. She had cooked at other camps. They stayed in their camp trailer while Ellis built them a cute two bedroom home. Our kids called them Honaker Man and Honaker Lady.

After ten years we began to feel restless and like we were ready for a change. Rusty was attending a school in Gallup for handicapped kids and we began to dream of having a ministry in the future for handicapped kids. A couple of times we had Rusty's school out to ride the horses.

While on a vacation trip to California we visited with a former UIM missionary, Allen Livingston. He was on the staff at North Valley Baptist in Redding, California and they were looking for a camp director for Lassen Pines Camp near Lassen National Park. We visited the camp and really like the area and the possibilities there.

When we got back to New Mexico we really struggled with the decision of leaving the mission. It was not an easy decision to make. God had used us to build the camp. The large multipurpose building was completed and ten cabins were constructed. We loved the folk at the ranch and our ministry there.

Steve had served as an interim pastor for a year at Gallup Baptist and really enjoyed it. Because of Rusty we also had this dream of sometime starting a home for handicapped people. We felt like we wanted to be closer to our families when we did that.

North Valley Baptist flew us to Redding for an interview with their board and the camp committee and we were unanimously accepted to direct Lassen Pines Camp in Shingletown. We prayed a lot and finally decided to take the position.

It was hard to pack up and move away from Summer Park Ranch and the staff there. It was hard to leave all our many friends at Gallup Baptist Church. And it was hard to leave all our dear friends with the United Indian Missions. But we were also excited about the move. We had seen Summer Park Ranch develop into a real camp.

Billy (who was now 18 years old) had found a job working as a janitor at the Gallup Hospital. We helped him find an apartment in Gallup that he shared with another young man who also worked at the hospital. He seemed quite happy with his independence and promised to keep in touch.

We brought Nugget, Pokey and Stormy (one of Nuggets colts) with us. Steve Diddams had recently gotten his driver's license so he drove our pick up truck for us. We had a rented U-Haul truck, our truck and our little jeep. We were quite a caravan.

We shed tears when we pulled out of the SPR entrance gate. We had ten years of wonderful memories and we had so many wonderful friends in the southwest.

Part IV

Shingletown Lassen Pines Camp and Open Door Community Church

Left, Lassen Pines Christian Camp Bible Hall

Below, a small lake on the camp property

Left, Lassen Pines Dining Hall

TWENTY

New Friends and Responsibilities

When we made the trip to Redding to interview for the position of Lassen Pines Director we had looked at a home for sale that was located near the camp. It had four large bedrooms and was a reasonable price. My Dad helped us put some money down on it.

There were so many changes. We went from a very arid dry climate to having a year round creek in our back yard. We went from new buildings that we had helped construct from the ground up to a beautiful but very old lodge that had been constructed in the 1920's. The plumbing was always clogging up or spurting up somewhere. One time a lady came up and asked me where the director was. I told her to look for the man with the plumber's helper.

We went from programming the camps and arranging the speakers ourselves to hosting different groups each week that brought their own program, speakers and counselors.

Our camp staff worked in the kitchen and dining room and kept the facilities clean. They also ran the snack shop.

Lassen Pines had two separate camps that ran each week in the summer.

The main camp had a beautiful old lodge that contained the kitchen and dining hall and upstairs rooms. There was several other lodges and cabins. The main camp had a capacity for about 150 people.

There was also a covered wagon camp at the other end of the property. It had 10 covered wagons for cabins. Each wagon had 5 bunk beds. There was an outside eating area and a circular area of log benches for meetings. There was a capacity for about 90 at the wagon camp.

Down at the covered wagon camp a huge statue of Paul Bunyan stood. It had been given to the camp by a restaurant in Redding that went out of business.

Campers at the main camp enjoyed a swimming pool that was 12 feet deep on one end with a high dive. It was the first time we had cared for a swimming pool so we had a lot to learn about chlorine levels and keeping a pool clean. We had one college age young man, Tom Kinnier, who handled the pool for us all summer. He was a certified life guard. Tom and his family became long time friends of ours.

Campers at the covered wagon camp enjoyed swimming in one of the two large ponds that were on the campgrounds. There were row boats available for both camps at the other pond.

Meals for both camps were prepared in the main dining hall. Meals were sent out to the wagon camp on a chuck wagon. California health department said that any food that left the main dining hall had to be destroyed if it was not eaten. So we had to be very careful in figuring the quantity of food sent in the chuck wagon. We had an excellent cook.

With the two camps going on at once, we had our hands full keeping everybody happy. Fortunately we had a great staff of teens.

When we moved to Shingletown Randy was 10, Rusty was 8 and Heidi was 6. They attended Black Butte School and quickly made new friends. Rusty went to kindergarten with Heidi.

Randy and Heidi always protected their brother. I remember (back in New Mexico) one time we had a couple of neighbor boys in our car who were teasing Rusty. Randy (who was 6 years old at the time) asked them, "Who gave you your mind?" When they answered that they guessed God had, Randy said, "Well did you get to choose a smart one?" After admitting they did not get that choice, they seemed to get the picture. I never heard them tease Rusty again.

That first year Rusty did fine in kindergarten with Heidi. The next year he attended a special education school in Redding. Since it was 40 miles away we only sent him three days a week. He rode the bus with the high school kids (who all had to go to Redding). Black Butte School in Shingletown only went to the eighth grade.

We attended North Valley Baptist Church in Redding on Sunday evenings. Steve was on their staff since they owned Lassen Pines.

North Valley Baptist was searching for a music minister. We knew that Tom Fox was looking for a change after his many years of service in Los Gatos and so Steve suggested him. The church called Tom to come to Redding and that was a real delight to us. We were able to fellowship with Tom and Barbara again.

Tom is the son of Dale Evans Rogers and all three of his daughters had helped us in our camping ministry (Mindy and Candy at Summer Park Ranch and now Julie was helping us at Lassen Pines).

Tom always has a group called the Sage Singers that he uses to lead a lot of the music. I was really thrilled and flattered when he asked me to be his fiddle player in the Sage Singers he started in Redding. Barbara played a melodica in the group. Allen Livingston sang with Tom and so did our cook, Ben, from Lassen Pines. And we had a great guitar player.

That was such a wonderful experience. I had played the violin for years but had always wanted to fiddle. Tom and Barbara taught me a lot. We led the music at North Valley Baptist every Sunday evening and also played at several special events in the Redding area.

Most Sunday mornings we were saying good bye to a weekend retreat we had just hosted. So we started attending the Open Door Community Church in Shingletown on Sunday mornings. It was a small fellowship of folk meeting in the home of Boyd and Coila Woodmansee. Their home was not far from the camp Their pastor, Dan O'Donnell, was a student at Shasta Bible College in Redding. He lived in Redding and drove up for Sunday mornings.

We really enjoyed the group of folk that attended Open Door Community Church. Some of them began to help us in the kitchen during the Fall, Winter and Spring months when we had a large camp in.

Many times after a weekend retreat we had leftovers that would spoil, so we would invite everyone over after church on Sunday to help us eat them up. And most would bring something from their kitchen to add to the meal. We had some great times. After enjoying the meal we would sing around the piano and visit. Some of the men had guitars and I had my fiddle.

We soon found out that being the host and hostess for a busy camp worked out much better with us having our living quarters on the campgrounds. Running back and forth continually from our home to the camp was hard on our family. We often stayed in one of the cabins at camp.

So we made an apartment out of the rooms that were above the Bible Hall (the old dance hall) for our family to live in. We converted one of the rooms into a small kitchen, and another into a cozy little living room, which left two bedrooms (one for Steve and I and one for Heidi) on the first floor. Rusty and Randy had a room that was on the peak of the building. They went up a little ladder from our hallway to their room. They really liked their hideout.

We rented our home to some folk and the rent helped to make the payments on the house.

Ten year old Randy enjoyed fishing in Bailey Creek which was right behind the camp. He would watch for the forest service fish truck to go by. Then he would run out and fish in the creek about a quarter of a mile downstream from where they dumped the fish. He also really enjoyed the high dive at the swimming pool. He and Heidi became excellent swimmers.

Rusty wore out two plastic big wheel tricycles whizzing around the tennis courts that were just below our apartment.

Heidi was the camp sweetheart. All the older gentlemen from camp and church fell in love with her.

My Uncle Bob had purchased about twenty acres in lower Shingletown years before. He let Steve fix the fence he had around his acreage and graze our horses there. One day (in the middle of camp season) we discovered that the horses had gotten loose and had been running around. By the time we discovered they were out they had been picked up by the sheriff's office and hauled to Redding to an animal shelter. Steve went to get them and found out that only Nugget and Pokey were there. Stormy was lost and no one seemed to know where he was.

Two and a half years later, Heidi had a school assignment to write a paper about an experience that made you sad. She wrote about losing Stormy. It was a real surprise to find out that her teacher's aide had found Stormy and had him in her corral at her house all this time. So Stormy returned, fat and sassy.

TWENTY-ONE

A Visit to Little Valley

The second summer that we were at Lassen Pines (1977) we had two teens on our staff that were from Ohio, Theresa and John Bolesky. Their folks had lived in Redding for a couple of years and had just moved back to Ohio. Theresa and John kept telling us about their Dad's ranch in Little Valley and wanted us to go see it.

Their Dad, John, Sr. had purchased a ranch in Little Valley sight unseen. The realtor had not been truthful with John. John wanted a ranch with a meadow and a creek and room for grazing cattle. That it had. But he was not informed of the dilapidated condition the buildings were in. And he was not told that there was not an adequate water supply on dry years for grazing very many cattle.

On Saturdays (after the campers had left and things were cleaned up) we were always looking for something fun to do with our staff. One Saturday afternoon we decided to take the crew to Little Valley to visit the Bolesky's ranch.

We traveled to the little town of McArthur and then turned south. We bumped along a red cinder road and passed picturesque ranches. We got into a country that reminded us of our days in the southwest. After leaving the ranches and civilization, sage brush and scrub oaks and a few pines dotted the landscape. We passed a huge old round barn that had been used in the past for training horses.

Finally (about 18 miles south of McArthur) we came to a railroad track. Just past the tracks was a Welcome to Little Valley sign that also read, " Where the Pavement Ends and the West Begins". That is exactly the feeling we had. When you crossed those tracks, you were entering a different era. Little Valley was quite rundown and the whole place had a ramshackled look. It was unique.

After driving past the little town we rounded the corner and got a glimpse of the valley. It was beautiful!

Then we drove into the ranch headquarters. The buildings were extremely run down. There was a lot of shacks that people were renting and living in. It was a mess. But we really liked the cookhouse (that had been used to feed the cowhands when it was a working ranch), the old bunkhouse (that in the past had housed the cowhands) and the dance hall (where in the past many fun times were held). There was even an old saloon. We found out later that the saloon was on the neighbor's property. They were quaint old buildings and were in still good condition. They were kept locked so no one used them. Clover Corder showed us through them.

The ranch land in the valley was gorgeous. Then we drove down past the valley, past a little dam and pond that irrigated the valley and came to Dixie Valley Ranch. There was a small part of land in Dixie Valley that was John's.

It was a fun outing. At the time we did not think much more about the place.

Open Door Community Church had a part time pastor, Dan O'Donnell. Dan and his family would drive up every Sunday from Redding, where he lived and was attending Shasta Bible College. Dan still had one school year left in Redding before he left for seminary. Steve began teaching the adult Sunday School class

The church was growing and had purchased property to build on. The folk asked Steve if he would consider being their pastor when Pastor Dan left for seminary. We were thoroughly enjoying the fellowship in Shingletown and could see such a potential for the church there. We had perfect peace when he told them that he would be happy to pastor the church when Dan left for seminary. However Steve did not feel right about attending there (as the next pastor) while Dan was still pastor. So we prayed about what we should do. We resigned the camp director position at Lassen Pines at the close of our second summer there.

TWENTY-TWO

A Restful Year in Millville

During that second summer John and Joyce Bolesky came out from Ohio to visit their kids. We immediately bonded with them. Our family and their family enjoyed a wonderful picnic out in the woods not far from Shingletown.

They owned a home in a community called Millville. Millville is located between Redding and Shingletown. The folk that were living in their home were moving out, so John and Joyce were looking for someone to move into it and care for it. We could move into their home for the coming school year and stay there until Dan left the church and went to seminary. And we could continue renting out our home up in Shingletown. It seemed like the perfect solution to their dilemma and ours.

We were pleasantly shocked when we saw the home. It was huge, beautiful and was fully furnished with lovely furniture. I was excited about the baby grand piano in the living room. Our kids were thrilled because for the first time in their lives they would have a television. And this TV was a big one with color. Steve was overjoyed that the home was on ten acres with a creek and a it had nice barn and corrals. So we even had a spot for Nugget and Polka Dotty.

Shortly before our move to Millville, Steve was picking up a load of groceries at the warehouse in Redding where we bought most of our food for camp. He mentioned to the manager that we would be leaving the camp in a few weeks and moving to Millville. He added that he was looking for work. The manager said they needed another truck driver and asked if he would work for them. So just like that he had a job.

Some other new friends, Bud and Leona Hennessey, were starting a church in Burney. We met them because their daughter, Ruth, worked on our staff at Lassen Pines. Bud asked Steve if he would consider driving up to Burney each Sunday to teach the adult Sunday School class. He agreed to do that.

As soon as our second summer at Lassen Pines was over we moved down to the Bolesky's gorgeous home in Millville. God had certainly provided a wonderful place for us while we waited for our new ministry up in Shingletown. We stored all of our furniture in their big garage.

Our kids were thrilled to find the home had a ski boat in the garage that the Bolesky's said we could use. Randy could hardly wait to try it out. One day shortly after we moved to Millville we took the boat to Shasta Lake.

We had never ever driven a ski boat before. Steve and the kids had not even been in one. Shortly after we put the boat in the lake (when Steve was still trying to get the engine started) I noticed the boat was filling with water. I yelled to Steve that we had a major leak. Some people in a boat next to us informed us to take the plug out of the steering wheel and put it in the hole that is in the back of the boat. Then realizing that we were totally new at boating, they nicely explained that the hole was to drain the water each time we finished for the day. The plug was stored in the steering wheel so you would be reminded to put it in the next time you got in the water.

After removing the boat and draining the water. We put in the plug and started over. What a great time we had! That was the first of many waterskiing trips.

A few years later we were able to trade a car (that Steve was given for a wedding he had) for an older boat. We spent many happy times camping and waterskiing with our kids and their friends at Whiskeytown Lake. All three of our kids became great water-skiers. It took a lot of hours of trying to get Rusty up, but Randy and Heidi were determined he could do it and so was he. What excitement for all of us when he finally stayed up. Once he caught on he became a good little water skier.

We registered Randy and Heidi in the Christian school at North Valley Baptist. They really liked it. Randy was in the 6th grade and Heidi was in the 2nd. They both made some really nice friends there. Rusty attended the special education school that he had been attending part time.

I was so excited when I went to register the kids for school and found that the school secretary was Marcy Caldwell. Years before, when we were on a deputation trip with the mission and staying with my parents, Steve went to a drug store in Los Gatos to get some medicine. He had Rusty with him. At the drug store he met a very sweet lady named Marcy. She told Steve that she had a little girl just like Rusty. So they chatted for awhile. The next morning when we put Rusty in the Jewels Sunday school class (the class that Calvary Church had for handicapped children) there was Marcy with her little girl, Lisa. So we all had a nice visit. Well here I was several years later in Redding chatting with Marcy again. She and her family had moved to Redding and she was the school secretary at North Valley Baptist Christian School. Rusty and Lisa were in the same class at the special Ed school.

Marcy and I became great friends. I was soon bored in the big house by myself each day after Steve left for work and the kids went to school. It did not take me long to put the dishes in the dish washer and tidy up the home. So I volunteered several days a week at the school. They assigned me to helping Jack George, the new music leader at North Valley Baptist. Tom Fox had left the staff of North Valley about the same time Steve did. I worked in the office right next to Marcy and also gave music lessons.

The Bolesky's had two horses on their ranch in Little Valley. They asked Steve if he would go to Little Valley and get them and keep them in Millville. So once again we made a trip to Little Valley and saw their ranch up there.

We enjoyed a good restful year in the home in Millville.

Above: Open Door Community Church, 1980
Left: Open Door Community Church, first building, 1978

TWENTY-THREE

First Years at Open Door Community Church and One Huge Lincoln Log Set

We were really excited about moving back up to Shingletown and Steve being the first full time pastor at the Open Door Community church. The area around Shingletown was really growing.

June 1978 (as soon as school was out) we moved back up to our home in Shingletown. There were two other small community churches in the Shingletown area. Shortly after Steve became the pastor both churches joined our fellowship. This was a wonderful answer to prayer. One of the groups had a small building on leased land in lower Shingletown. The Open Door Fellowship had five acres in upper Shingletown and no building yet. So we moved that building up to the church property.

Right away the men added Sunday school rooms on to the building. They filled up quickly. The small sanctuary was so full that oftentimes Steve and I would take turns with one seat on the front row. He sat in it while I played the piano for the song service and I sat in it while he preached. We did not have any kitchen facilities. So a new auditorium was soon added which more than doubled the size of the building. The men made a kitchen and Sunday school classrooms in the old part of the building.

The new addition also contained a nice office for Steve and one for a secretary. Carol Thompson became Steve's secretary. That was wonderful. I had been typing the Sunday bulletins and the Shingle Jingle (our church newsletter) in our home and ran them off on an old mimeograph we had set up in our garage. Carol was a great secretary.

A lot of my family was moving to the area My Uncle Bob (my Mom's brother) had built a home on acreage he had purchased in lower Shingletown quite a few years before we moved to Lassen Pines. He was still living in Alameda.

My Uncle Johnny and Aunt Grace had purchased some of his property and moved up along with my Mom's parents, Grandma and Grandpa Weller. My Uncle Dick and Aunt Nancy were also moving to Shingletown. (We had never lived near so much family).

Shortly after we made our move back to Shingletown, my Dad retired from over 30 years of service at Calvary Church in Los Gatos. Dad and Mom desired to retire up near us and the rest of the family. So when they sold their home in Los Gatos they moved in with us. Our home had four large bedrooms, so we gave Dad and Mom the big master bedroom. We had a large garage that we stored their belongings in.

Together we purchased five acres of property near Lake McCumber. Dad made plans to build a small two bedroom home for he and Mom. Steve and I ordered a log home.

The property was on Eagle Lane. About ¼ mile from our land there was a huge bald eagle's nest. We all enjoyed watching the bald eagle. But that eagle became a real problem. The Department of Fish and Game decided that the county should have never sold us the land to build on because the eagle's nest was too close. So we could not get our building permits.

There were several others who had purchased property on Eagle Lane. Fortunately some were much more boisterous and pushy than us and actual threats were made to the eagle's life. The county finally decided that they would have to issue building permits to us because they had let us purchase the property for homes. (We wondered why they took awhile to come to that conclusion).

Meanwhile back at our house, my Dad built all the cupboards for both of our homes in our garage. He knew that we would be building somewhere.

It was very exciting the day our logs were delivered from Montana. A lot of the men from the church came to help unload. It was not a large home (24' x 44'). It would have two small bedrooms and a bathroom downstairs with a loft above them. It had an open kitchen, dining room and living room. As they were emptying all the logs from the truck one of the men said he was sure that the front of the truck was in Redding.

Our pile of logs was like a huge Lincoln log set. Each log had a letter and a number on it. Steve had the directions for where each log went. He would yell out the next numbers. Heidi and I would find them as Randy and Steve lugged them over and fastened them down to the growing home.

Our logs were specially made with a hole bored down the center of each log. This was to alleviate them from splitting and to help with the wiring. While they were sitting in the woods waiting to be set in place, we soon found out that the center hole made wonderful nests for some unwanted neighbors. Scorpions! Heidi and I became very efficient at searching for scorpions and killing them with spray cans of bug killer.

Several of the retired men from the church came often and helped with the construction of our home. And some of the college age guys who had helped us at Lassen Pines came up to help.

Dad hired a young man, Don Geeter, to help him full time. Don was a great builder and fun to be with. He and his wife, Sharon, became good friends. They were members of our church and only lived about a mile from us.

It was late spring so we camped on the property while we were building. As soon as the logs were up and the roof was on we put our couch (which was a hide-a-bed) out on the big front porch. The porch went along the whole front of the cabin. The kids had mattresses and sleeping bags. It was a great family time for us—chatting with the kids each night as we watched the stars come out.

We went to Lassen Pines several times a week to use their shower rooms. We had our washing machine in a shed we had built on the property and used the generator to wash clothes.

Mom and Dad moved my Grandpa and Grandma's camper to the place and lived in it.

A group called Lights Ministries had moved to Lassen Pines. They were now running the camps. Some friends from Redding purchased our Viola home and rented it to the director of Lights Ministries. That was sure an answer to prayer.

Several of the folk from Light Ministries joined our church fellowship and were a real asset.

We moved into our homes several months before electricity was available in our area. We used lanterns at night, had large ice chests in our kitchens and cooked on our propane camp stoves. Dad had purchased a generator for building, so every Saturday morning he turned it on and made waffles for all of us. They were a real treat. The generator came in handy any time we really needed electricity.

Our good friends and neighbors, Ben and Teddy Ostarello, made ice for our ice chests and helped us in so many ways. Don and Bev Cole and Don and Maxine Ross also lived close and helped us a lot. Uncle Johnny also came up almost every day to help.

What a celebration we had the day the electricity was connected to our homes. It was funny to see what each of us enjoyed the most. It was impossible for me to decide whether I enjoyed the water, the stove or the refrigerator the most.

We had never had a television set (accept in the Bolesky's home) so that was not an issue. The folks had one so the kids started going over to their home for Bonanza and Little House on the Prairie. I usually went over on Saturday evenings for Lawrence Welk.

Mom and I cleared a lot of underbrush that was in a thick grove of pine trees on the property between our homes. We put picnic tables in there and

The King's log cabin on Eagle Lane

named it King-Kee park (for the Kings and McKees). We had a lot of fun picnics and church potlucks in King-Kee park.

McCumber Lake was just down the road from us. So often on hot summer afternoons the three kids and I would walk to the lake. Rusty learned to swim there. Randy and Heidi had become excellent swimmers while we were at Lassen Pines. I enjoyed floating on an inner tube or reading on the shore while they played.

Right across McCumber Lake from us was a Boy Scout camp that was used for a camp for handicapped children one week every year. We sent Rusty there one year. We were afraid he might get homesick some day and decide to hike home. But he didn't. He had a great time.

Some of our very best friends, who were members of our church, Dave and Nancy George, had purchased five acres right across from us. They built a huge log home. Dave and Steve bought a milk cow together that we named King George. We had a pen and a little shed for her near our log home.

The guys took turns milking her. Randy ended up doing a lot of the milking. It was about the time that Randy had started singing, so we could hear him singing (at the top of his lungs) out in the woods to the cow. She must have enjoyed it because she always gave a lot of milk.

When we had the cow in New Mexico I had learned to make butter and cottage cheese. I don't think store bought cottage cheese is near as good as home made. Homemade cottage cheese has a squeak to it when you eat it. We made butter by shaking the cream in a jar. We would make a family game of passing the jar around and the winner was the one who was shaking when the butter finally came.

We also had a few chickens. Heidi had a pet chicken she named Henrietta. It would follow her when she let it out of the pen and liked it when she carried her around.

Royce and Marge Rickman came out to visit and brought Heidi a Morgan horse named Chiquita. Heidi had Chiquita for years. She died shortly after Heidi was married. Randy had Pokey and of course we had Nugget. Steve usually had a horse he was training for someone.

Besides building their log home, Dave and Nancy were also building a home on their property for Nancy's parents, Lloyd and Gladys Usrey. So my parents really enjoyed the fellowship of the Usrey's. Mom and Gladys enjoyed taking a walk together every afternoon.

Billy had gotten a wonderful job working for the railroad. He worked with a crew that fixed the tracks. Every so often he would get a break and pop in on us. We never knew when that one be.

Once while in the log home Heidi was having a slumber party with a few of her friends. After a fun time in the evening we had all settled down for the night. The girls were all in sleeping bags in the living room. All of a sudden one of them screamed. Billy had arrived unannounced and was peaking in the window to see if he should just sneak in and sleep on the couch like he usually did. When the girl saw a very dark man with long dark hair looking in the window she imagined the worst!

Heidi quietly explained, "That's my brother Billy." We got him settled in

Randy's room. Randy had an older model one bedroom trailer home behind our house for his room. (At the time of this writing, Billy is still working for the railroad and he still pops in on us). We always enjoy his visits.

For one family vacation while we were at the log home, we went on a three day and night camping trip on horseback. Randy was on Pokey. Steve rode a horse he was training for someone. Rusty was on Nugget. Heidi had Chiquita and I was on a white mule named Pinkey. Pinky belonged to the Rasters (friends who lived near us and attended our church). She was white and had pink eyes. She had a habit of lagging way behind and then trotting to catch up with the rest.

We sure had a great time out in the woods alone as a family. We camped each night by a creek. It was so quiet and we did not have to spend a dime on gasoline, motels or even campsites. And we did not see a single soul (besides us) on the whole trip.

Pastors are dealing with people constantly every day. They get tired and their families get tired of sharing them. So that was a very special trip for all of us.

Another year, for a different vacation, we rented a motor home. We were going to visit Yosemite and Lake Tahoe. Steve had just brought the motor home to our home from Redding and Rusty was so excited. While we were loading up the motor home, Rusty leaped off the top of the steps that went up to the loft in our log home. He broke a bone in his foot. Our first stop the next morning was to the doctor. Once Rusty had the cast on it, he felt much better. So at Yosemite, every time we went for a long hike, we rented a donkey (named Festus) for Rusty to ride on. It worked great.

Uncle Johnny gave Randy a small motor cycle. Randy was thrilled. We did not want him on the paved roads but around our place there was miles of dirt roads and trails he could ride on. His favorite jaunt was from our cabin to the little Shingletown airport. There was one airplane that someone from Shingletown kept there. Randy visited that plane every time he could. Oftentimes another plane would be there. He would come back and tell us details about the planes.

In his bedroom he had a big poster of the inside of a jet cockpit.

In the winter months the kids had great times with snow mobiles. We did not own one but some of our church folks did and made them available to our kids. Randy had two at his disposal and he thoroughly enjoyed them.

Our kids really enjoyed the many retired folk at the church.. They were so good to the kids. Once one of Randy's schoolmates asked him why his best friends were all old men. Randy teasingly told him, he liked the price of their toys, but he really enjoyed their friendship.

Sometimes on Saturday afternoons Clarence Mullins (a retired man) would call and ask if Randy would come over Sunday after church and play with him. Randy would have lunch with Clarence and his wife, MaryJane, at their home and then play guitar with him. Joe Hiatt (another retiree) would join them with his guitar.

Don Ross would have him over to talk airplanes. Don was a retired TWA airlines pilot. (Don was best man in Randy's wedding years later).

Heidi was their little sweetheart. Earl Stanley, another one of our retirees, told her that before she married he had to check the guy out.

And of course Rusty wiggled his way into everyone's heart. He had a special lady friend who for some reason he always called Charlie Brown. She lived about a mile from us. She was so happy that he thought of her as special that she never minded being called Charlie Brown.

One day we discovered that Rusty was missing. He was mad at something and decided to run away to Charlie Brown's. He had packed a little bag and taken off without our knowing. Charlie was so happy that he had come to her house. She let us know immediately that he was there. So after awhile we went and got him and by then he was quite happy and ready to come back.

There is one night that we will never forget. It was really cold! McCumber lake was frozen over. The ground was covered with snow.

I heard a howling. It really sounded frightening. The kids and I decided to go investigate. Steve was at a church board meeting.

We followed the howling to the lake and there we saw, Frosty, one of the George's beautiful Siberian husky dogs. He had fallen through the ice. All we could see was his wet head poking up through the ice about 30 feet out from the shore. We rushed back to Nancy's. (Dave was at the church board meeting with Steve).

We decided that Randy and Nancy would have to crawl out on the ice very flat (like inchworms) so as not to break the ice. Then they would put a rope around Frosty's neck and front lets and then we would all try to pull him out while laying flat. Brrr!

So we quickly layered up and drove back to the lake. Then they did their inchworm crawl out to Frosty. Randy and Nancy managed to get the rope around him. They both reached in as low as possible and we all really pulled. It was not fun. But it was exciting and it did work! We pulled poor Frosty to safety!

After they carefully crawled on top of the ice back to shore, we all quickly rushed back for hot showers.

Pastor Steve, Open Door Community Church

TWENTY-FOUR

The Lord's Blessings on Church and Family

The church was really growing and the Lord was blessing our fellowship. New folk were coming and souls were being saved. The new addition to our building was full every Sunday morning and the folk started making plans for another addition.

When we first started at the church, as a family we cut and sold firewood to supplement our income. Gradually we had to sell less and less wood. And it was not long before we were able to quit selling wood.

Steve usually rode one of our three horses to church each day. He had a path through the trees. One of our members told us that someone told him that it looked like our pastor was never at the church. He seldom saw a car there. The member replied, "Just look in the trees for his horse."

Steve was very busy planning messages for three services a week (Sunday morning and evening and Wednesday evening). On Wednesday evenings after the Bible study many folk stayed after for choir practice. For years Clyde Van Wagner directed our choir and later Frank Algarme moved up and he became our director. We often did a cantata for Christmas and Easter. They were a lot of fun.

For several years on Easter Sunday our church would go up to Lassen Pines for an Easter Sunrise service (outside by the lake if it was nice or inside Bible Hall if it was too chilly). Then we would have a great breakfast in the dining hall, followed by our morning service in Bible Hall. Tom Smith was the cook and he could prepare a scrumptious meal.

I enjoyed singing in a trio with Ellie Hyatt and Maxine Ross. All three of us were under five feet tall. Our favorite song was one of Evie's that went "I'm four feet eleven, on my way to heaven and I feel like I'm ten feet tall!"

I remember one Wednesday evening after a midweek service there was a bear in the parking lot. That made for some excitement.

With so many new subdivisions in Shingletown a lot of our new members were building homes. Whenever time allowed, Steve enjoyed helping folk with their building projects.

With so many of our members being retirement age, he made a lot of trips to Redding for hospital visits. Poor Steve. He has always hated hospitals. When he visits people and sees them sick he often gets squeamish. Twice he fainted while visiting folk in the hospital.

The last few years that my Dad was on the staff at Calvary Church in Los Gatos he headed up a senior ministry. They had a monthly fellowship and he took the seniors on a bus tour each year. So when they moved to Shingletown he started an "Over 50" ministry at our church. They had a monthly fellowship that was very popular and he started some regular outings. He also arranged several bus tours. He never had any trouble getting enough reservations to fill the bus.

Steve and I were able to go along (even thought we were not yet over 50) on two of the tours. We enjoyed helping with the luggage and hosting everyone. Steve gave a short devotional on the bus each day. It was a lot fun and a good way to get to really know folk.

One year we had a Canyonlands Tour. It included Zion and Bryce National Parks and the Grand Canyon. We especially enjoyed visiting the southwest again.

The other tour we took was to Victoria, Canada.

We will never forget one of the nights on that trip. It was dark and pouring down rain and one of our elderly ladies tripped and fell in the parking lot while she was walking from the bus to the motel. Her top layer of false teeth fell out and broke into pieces. She was devastated! Well, Steve has an upper plate himself. I always traveled with plate weld in our overnight bag because once he had them break and I feared it might happen again.

So Steve and I found all of the pieces of her teeth in the puddle (out in the parking lot with a flashlight in the pouring down rain). We took them up to the lady's room where Steve carefully glued all the pieces back together. It took a couple of hours. She was overjoyed and the teeth actually stayed together until she got back to Shingletown and saw her dentist. The dentist could not believe what a marvelous job Steve had done on those teeth.

Shortly after we moved back to Shingletown, Steve was appointed to the Black Butte School Board to fill a vacancy. Then he was elected to the Board in the next two elections. He served on the school board for six years. The principal at Black Butte School all those years was Charlie Menoher, who later became the Superintendent of Schools for Shasta County. Steve really enjoyed working with Charlie.

One summer I worked with the church kids to perform a little musical called "Down by the Creek Bank". We would work on it while the parents were having Wednesday Bible Study. Randy's part (the old bull frog) had an almost two octave range and he shocked me by singing it without straining on the highs or the lows. I took him to the little organ we had in our cabin and played a scale for him to sing. He sang deep bass notes that most men would not be able to hit and then could go up two octaves from there.

Randy had taken some guitar lessons and loved entertaining us with Johnny Cash songs.

Shortly after our musical, we had a special singer, Mike Shea, come to the church and sing. During our singing time, Randy was belting out the songs in the front row from his hymn book (like he always did) and Mike noticed. He told us after the service that if we were interested he would like to start giving Randy some voice lessons. So he started voice lessons with Mike. Mike had

Randy sing special numbers with him at several of the local churches and he even took him down to the Bay Area to sing.

Then when Randy was in high school Frank Algarme moved to Shingletown and started leading music at our church. Frank had a wonderful bass baritone voice and had done a lot of singing. He was going to be singing in a musical at Shasta College so suggested Randy try out for a part. Randy got a good part in the musical "The Little Sweep".

He loved it and learned so much that we let him try out the next year when the college performed La Boehme. Singing became his passion and opera was his favorite style. His high school buddies thought he was nuts and even we were a bit surprised when Pavarotti became his favorite singer.

He was able to sing supporting roles in "The Little Sweep", "La Boehme" and "Amaul and the Night Visitors" at Shasta College. At Shasta County music camps he was Curly in "Oklahoma" and sang in "Annie Get Your Gun."

TWENTY-FIVE

Mountain Jewels Home Begins

When Randy was a sophomore in high school and Heidi was in the sixth grade we registered them in Liberty Christian school We heard that they had a good music group, Liberty Singers, and we had heard good things in general about Liberty Christian. Both kids loved their teachers and their new friends they made at Liberty.

The first time after that when Steve went to Black Butte School to visit with Charlie Menoher about something, Charlie expressed his disappointment in Steve putting Heidi in a private school. Steve explained that he felt like he still had a lot of kids at Black Butte. About then several kids came running up, gave Steve a hug and said, "Hi, Pastor Steve!" Charlie grinned and said, "I see what you mean."

We were happy to learn that Heidi's teacher was to be Larry MacClanahan. Larry was a Navajo from Window Rock who had often spoken at Summer Park Ranch for us in New Mexico. Larry attended Bob Jones University and there he met Linda who was from the Redding area. They married and after living in Window Rock, Arizona for awhile they moved to Anderson, California.

Every so often I would make Navajo fry bread and send some with Heidi for Larry. In this case, fry bread was much better than "apples for the teacher".

Rusty was in the Special Education School in Redding.

All three kids had to make the 45 mile commute each school day, so I was happy to find a part time job from 9:00 a.m. to 2:00 p.m. each day in Redding. Our friend and neighbor Teddy Ostarello helped me get the job.

After working for about a year and a half, the company I was working for had to downsize and I was out of a job. Fortunately Randy now had his driver's license.

For a long time Steve and I had been talking about taking in another child who was mentally handicapped like Russ. So when I lost my job (and I really needed to work to supplement our income) we called the county and attended the next class they had for regulations of group homes.

We found out that in order to get just one child you had to have the same license and training for a home for six children.

At the training meeting we met friends from Shingletown, Chuck and Andra McLucas. They had just built a huge home near our home in Viola with a group home in mind. They were interested in taking in girls who were in trouble.

We sat with them during the session. By the end of the training session they had changed their mind about having a home because of all the regulations and restrictions. They had two children still at home. And we had learned our little log cabin was too small to get another child. The McLucas's asked us if we would consider leasing their home for a group home.

We went to visit their home and could not believe it. It was huge! It was a three story home with six bedrooms. The bottom floor had a large kitchen and a huge living room, a bedroom and a office. Two huge staircases went upstairs from either side of the big entry way. There was five bedrooms on the second floor. The master bedroom was mammoth. It had a fireplace and the closet was as big as one of our bedrooms. There was a big hot tub in the master bath and also a shower room. The master bedroom also had a large deck off of it that overlooked the forest. The third floor was a large recreation room with a pool table and a ping pong table. They said that the ping pong table and pool table stayed with the home. The home had 6,000 square feet.

It was definitely a perfect set up for a group home and the MacLucas's were willing to let us be in it rent free until we were able to get some residents. But we had Mom and Dad living next to us on property we had purchased together and a little log cabin that we loved. And Steve had a full time ministry with a growing church. We did not have that large of a home in mind. And we were beginning to feel like all we did was move!

We did much praying and talked with Mom and Dad. Dad and Mom did not want to stand in our way if the Lord was in this decision to start a home for handicapped young people. I had been working for two years clear down in Redding so the thought of having a full time job right in my own house did sound great to me. Randy and Heidi were excited about the possibilities.

With a little fear and trepidation we made the decision to move to the MacLucas home and start proceedings to get a license for a home for handicapped kids. We had to name it for the licensing papers so we called it Mountain Jewels Home. The folk at Open Door Community Church were very supportive and gave us a shower for the home.

My Mom's parents and my Aunt Grace and Uncle Johnny had moved to lower Shingletown and had quite a few acres. They had purchased property from my Uncle Bob. He had bought quite a bit of property in Shingletown years ago. Dad decided he could move their home right next to my Grandparents home and help care for Grandma. Grandpa had just passed away and Grandma was happy to have my Mom next door. They purchased a few acres from her.

House movers sawed my parents home into two pieces and they moved it next to my Grandma's home. We put the log cabin and the five acres up for sale.

We had a good lawyer friend, Al Cunningham, who advised us to become incorporated as a nonprofit corporation and helped us with the paperwork for that. Chuck MacLucas was a Certified Public Accountant and later helped us get paperwork through the state for the nonprofit status. In years to come we became more and more thankful for the professional help of those two men. God was caring for us.

The first Mountain Jewels Hom in Shingletown.

We had many mixed emotions when we moved out of our little log home. It reminded us of when we moved from Summer Park Ranch. This time we were only moving a few miles down the road and we were moving from a tiny little home into a huge place. But we all really loved that little log home. And we knew we would never again experience the cozy family feeling we had there. But we knew we must be feeling the call of God. It is definitely hard to explain.

TWENTY-SIX

Busy Days, Full Lives

At the same time we decided to start Mountain Jewels Home, a lady, Carol Valles, from my brother Tom's church in Rancho Cordova came to him for some counsel. She mentioned that she was looking for help for her 17 year old son, Tom. He was developmentally disabled and she was looking for a Christian home for him. She was a single mother and had two daughters just older than Tom. She was looking for a good male influence for him. So Tom arranged for her to come up and meet us.

We fell in love with Carol and Tom right away. Tom moved in with us shortly after we moved. He rode the special-Ed bus to school every day with Russ. They shared a room and became great friends. At the time of this writing (27 years later), Tom is still living in Mountain Jewels Home.

Carol was the first secretary for the Mountain Jewels Home Corporation. Don Ross was our first vice president.

We never knew what Rusty and Tom would think up together. One day they came downstairs to show us what they had done to Rusty' brand new jacket. They had made it into a motorcycle jacket by painting stripes on the sleeves and numbers on the back with a red paint they had found in the garage. They were so thrilled with it and I was horrified. It was ruined!

Tom and Rusty, the first two of the MJR gang, October 1984

Another day Steve and I were both away when the school bus dropped the boys off. They decided they did not like being alone. Russ was 15 and Tom was 17 and they were both quite capable of being alone for a little while. But they decided to take the church directory and see if anyone knew where we were. They started in the A's and had gotten to the M's by the time we got home. We had visits and calls from a lot of folk that afternoon. Actually the folk all thought it was quite funny, but Steve and I did not. We certainly made sure we were home before their bus arrived after that.

It did not take us long to get all the paperwork finished and become a licensed home. The Regional Center immediately started sending children to us from families who needed a break. We always had one or two besides Russ and Tom. Randy and Heidi were my right hand helpers.

Our first resident from the Regional Center was a little guy who was five years old. He was tiny and looked to be about three. We had one of our bedrooms that was still totally empty. His mom told me she thought he would be the most happy (and the safest) playing in that empty room. She said if I would put some thongs (those rubber beach shoes) in it for him, he would be delighted. She had brought several pairs. She was right. He was perfectly content sitting on the floor with those flip flops, and was quite discontent with anything else. He would scoot them along the floor like they were cars. He would chew them and rub them and would bang them on his chin. We put a crib in there for his naps and night times and we hooked up an inner com so we could hear him when he was alone in the room.

His Mom had also told me that he liked to stick his head into round dark places. Once we found him in the fireplace with his head up the chimney (fortunately it was summer and the fireplace did not have ashes in it) . A few times he had his head in the toilet and another time he put his head in the wheel well of the truck. I was very relieved when our week with him was over. He was a sweet little guy but we had to have a constant watch on him, which was not easy in our huge home. With so much forest around I was tempted to put a leash on him when he went outside.

Then we got a 14 year old girl who was 6'2" tall. She was mentally handicapped and had epilepsy. Under control she only had one or two seizures daily. Every few weeks she would have a lot of seizures. Her mom was a really sweet lady and just needed a break. She thought that Kari would be fine for the two weeks we were to have her. Every two weeks the medicine would wear off and she would go into a period of almost constant seizures.

Kari loved me and loved to lean on me and give me hugs. Since she was almost a foot and half taller than me, we made quite a sight when Heidi and I took her shopping in Redding one day. She had a seizure in the mall and we got through that okay. Fortunately we were in Penney's between several racks of clothes. I do not think anyone saw us waiting for the seizure to subside. And then when Heidi and I took her to MacDonald's she wanted the toy that the little boy sitting in the next booth had. She tried to take it and started crying very loudly for it. It is not our practice to give someone what they want when the cry, but in this case I made an exception. I told Heidi to quickly go to the counter and try to get one of those toys. She calmed right down with the toy.

About this time we had our niece, Karen, who was the same age as Heidi, come down to help us for the summer. Heidi, Karen and Kari all donned their swimming suits and enjoyed the hot tub each day. Kari loved it. But one day Heidi yelled at me from upstairs to let me know Kari was having a seizure in the tub. She and Karen were able to keep her head above the water. We got her out when the seizure subsided but we decided we better forego the hot tub for Kari.

Peggy and Kari.

After a week she started having several seizures a day so I called her Mom and she came right up to get her. She said that the medicine would build up in her system and then quit working. My heart really went out to her Mom. We hoped that we were able to give her a little break.

Then we got a very rambunctious fourteen year old girl that was never still a minute. She ran from morning to night. She loved to pick me wildflowers from the yard. I had wildflower bouquets all over the house. Randy, Heidi, Karen and I took her and a couple of others on a long hike one day at Lassen National Park. That kept her quite busy that day. We came home with a lot of wild flowers.

About the same time we had her we got a little boy with Downs Syndrome. He was really cute but quite a handful. He had been in school with Rusty so we knew the family. We assigned Randy to him full time. He was so cute that everyone who saw him told him that he was cute. Randy taught him to say, "I'm not cute, I'm mean and ugly." At church he was saying that a lot. He was with us on our Lassen Park hike.

One of the girls we got had autism. She just wanted to rock in a rocking chair all day and kind of stared into space. Every now and then she would scream very loudly. We had a porch swing on our back deck that she was quite content in during the day. She just wanted to sit and swing. And then every so often she shrieked. She was a beautiful girl, but I could not take her anywhere because of the shrieking. Randy discovered she loved it when he blew in her face. Whenever he came by she would jump up and put her face next to his and make motions for him to blow.

I was talking to my mom on the phone one day when she was swinging out on the porch. She had swung out there for so many hours that one of the screws came loose from the roof. When the swing fell, she just quietly got up, came into the house and started rocking in the rocking chair.

We had gotten one full time resident besides Tom. Laura (I changed the name) was a teenage girl who came from a very wild background. She did not want to go to church and the social worker told us that we could not make her go.

Debbie, when we first started the adult care home.

TWENTY-SEVEN

Change to an Adult Care Home

Well, needless to say we were all getting exhausted. This life was not at all what we had in mind. I very seldom got to church. Fortunately one of the ladies from Lights Ministries was an excellent piano player and now played for our church services.

Then the director of the Shepherd's Home in Wisconsin came to speak at North Valley Baptist Church. The Shepherd's Home is a large Christian home for the developmentally disabled. We went to hear him and visited with him. He advised us to change our license to an adult home. He told us that most Christian families keep their handicapped children home with them until they are adults. The real need for Christian families was for adult care. He also advised us to be a private home and not accept government funding.

His advice was exactly what we had been praying about doing. Tom was about to turn 18 years old. We had talked with our good friends, Ken and Helen Kinnier, who had two handicapped adults. They were really interested in placing their daughter, Kaylynn, with us.

We had just recently met Gene and Nelle Nicolet who very much wanted us to take their daughter, Debbie, who had Downs Syndrome. Debbie was almost 30 years old.

So we went to the Regional Center and told them that we were changing our license with the state to a home for adults. We also mentioned that we already had three clients ready to sign up for our home and we had decided that we did not want to be licensed through them. We wanted to work privately with the parents. Steve thanked them for all their help. They were quite shocked that we were not dependent on their financial help. We did not want it.

We made a trip to Sacramento and changed the paperwork. The next week Debbie and Kaylynn moved in. It was wonderful. They fit right into our home and life style. Our lives returned to a somewhat normal schedule. All three of our residents were raised in the church and thoroughly enjoyed our busy church schedule.

Tom and Rusty went to school each morning. Kaylynn and Debbie helped me with housework and laundry in the huge home. Things were going really well.

Then one morning we had a visit from the State Fire Inspector. He told us that we could not have any of our clients in the upstairs bedrooms because of fire code. Without the five bedrooms on the second floor we were really hampered.

We immediately moved Tom and Rusty into the office room downstairs and Debbie and Kaylynn had to share the other downstairs bedroom. We had three empty bedrooms upstairs that we could not use and the downstairs was full.

The next week the folk who had purchased our home in Viola called. Lights ministry was moving from Lassen Pines so they no longer had renters in the home they had purchased from us. They had heard our plight and wondered if we were interested in buying it back.

Our old home had four large bedrooms. They told us that if we bought the home back they would help us financially to convert the garage into a big family room and help us add a garage with an upstairs apartment for Steve and I and our kids. Again we had an answer to our prayers. But I sure did not relish moving again. (Fortunately every time we moved in Shingletown we were able to keep our same address). That was sure a blessing.

My father and Uncle Johnny came up faithfully every morning and worked on making our garage into a large family room. We put knotty pine on the walls and carpeted the floor. We put a large wood stove in it with rock work underneath it and behind it. It was really nice. As soon as the living room addition was finished, once again we moved back to our original Shingletown house.

The home had four bedrooms. Steve and I had the master bedroom, Tom and Rusty shared a room. Heidi and Kaylynn shared a room and Debbie had her own room. Randy slept in our camper outside. He was headed off for college soon.

The kitchen was crowded with our big table, but it was fun. My Dad and Dick MacBride (a cabinet maker from our Shingletown church) had built us a beautiful table when we moved into the first home. The top was made with inlaid hardwood flooring and it had ceramic tile down the center. It is ten feet long so a gang can sit around it. It is also very sturdy. (It is still in beautiful shape).

Then we started the addition alongside our house that consisted of a garage downstairs and rooms upstairs. We built a staircase from our living room to the upstairs. Upstairs was two small bedrooms, an office and a bathroom. We hired one carpenter (a man from our church) fulltime and each day we usually had several other helpers. Uncle Johnny was so faithful to come every day.

As soon as we had the addition finished we added two more residents.

Randy was working nights at KVIP (the Redding Christian radio station). People often called the radio station for advice when they needed help from other Christians. One day a lady called and asked if KVIP knew of a Christian home for mentally challenged young people. She had a handicapped son and they were looking for a home for him. Since Randy often told the KVIP gang about our troop, they just happened to know of a home that was looking for another young man. The Lord sure had his hand in that one.

So Dick and Joyce Stark came out the next weekend and brought Bob. We had a nice visit with them and invited Bob up to stay for a couple of weeks. We immediately fell in love with Bob and the Starks. Bob has lived us ever since.

Bob is very quiet and shy. Fortunately he immediately bonded with Randy. They were soon teasing and joking all they time. I knew that he was really feeling at home when I found him hiding in a closet, knocking on the wall to tease me.

A man from the Redding newspaper came out and did an article on our home. Jeff Gilman, who was the director of the Redding Rescue Mission, read the article. He had taken a young man "under his wing" named Jim. Jim had come into the Portland Rescue Mission when Jeff and his wife, Debbie, were working there.

Jim had grown up in a foster home and when he turned 18 years old he was out of the system and on the his own. He had always attended special education classes in school. He joined the Navy. After a few weeks in the Navy he was discharged and out on the streets again. While living under a freeway bridge in Portland he came into the Rescue Mission. They realized he was a young man who needed help and took him in.

Jeff and Kathy were attending Multnomah Bible College and working at the mission. Jeff took a real liking to Jim and brought him down with him to Redding when he graduated from Multnomah and came to serve at the Redding Rescue Mission. When he noticed the article about our home he thought that maybe it would be a good fit for Jim.

I had a funny experience when I went to the mission to meet Jim. When I arrived at the mission I was greeted by a huge black man whose name was James. I did not mind at all him being black, but I wondered how in the world I would ever be able to feed him. And I wondered if we would need to get a bigger bed. He must have weighed close to 300 pounds. When I told him why I had come, he said, "Oh, you want to see Jimmy. I'll go get him." What a relief!

Jim really loved horses and loved the country. He was a perfect fit for us. So now we had Jim, Bob, Tom , Debbie and Kaylynn and of course, Rusty.

They all really fit into our family well. They enjoyed the church and were fun to have.

TWENTY-EIGHT

Israel Trip, Church Growth and Never a Dull Moment in Mountain Jewels Home

The church was still really growing. We were packing out the last addition. One of our newer members, Bill Hill, came to Steve and said that he had figured out how we could over double the size of the sanctuary. Bill was a fantastic carpenter and has since made a full time job of building churches. He had figured out how they could put a huge beam in to carry the load and add on to the existing building.

The men looked at his plans and were excited. So once again we were adding on to the church. One wonderful thing about all of the building we did at Open Door Community Church was that we never had to take out a loan. The Lord and God's people always provided the necessary funds.

Once when the men were working on the building a gentleman stopped. He had been watching the work and asked a few questions. Then he said that he would like to give us a piece of property that he had near McCumber lake. He said the church could sell it and use the money toward the construction costs.

About then the church gave Steve and I a trip to Israel as a gift. It was a special tour for pastors and their wives. My folks graciously volunteered to stay in our home and watch the gang while we were gone. I probably would not have gone if we did not have 17 year old Randy and 13 year old Heidi to help them. Heidi had Kaylynn in her room and was so good with her. They guys all loved Randy and responded very well to him.

We learned so much on our trip to Israel and it was really fun to be away with other pastors and their wives for the two weeks.

We flew from Los Angeles to London first. London had so many fascinating things to see. Between the jet lag and the damp cold of London, I came down with a horrible cold. So by the time we arrived in Israel I had a fever and was coughing and coughing. I had to spend one day recuperating in our hotel room. It was really scary to be in a foreign country, to not speak the language and be alone in the room all day. I was so glad to see Steve that evening.

Steve learned a lot from being there. He really enjoying going to Pilot's hall and walking the streets that Jesus walked. He was fascinated by visiting the kibbutzes and seeing how they grew their agriculture.

We both really enjoyed going to the Sea of Galilee and we really enjoyed visiting the garden of Gethsemane and going into the empty tomb. We had a wonderful prayer and praise service at the empty tomb.

Shortly after we returned to Shingletown from our trip we got a call from Connie Lemos. He had just heard of our home. They (Connie and Sissy) had a nineteen year old son, Clyde, who has Downs Syndrome. They wondered if we were interested in another young man. We had room for one more. So we arranged for Connie and his wife, Sissy, to bring Clyde up for a visit. Well, we fell in love with all of them and arranged for Clyde to come for a trial visit.

Clyde was a lot of fun and we all loved him. He moved in. Then we had our six we were licensed for—Tom, Kaylynn, Debbie, Jim, Bob and Clyde. We were to have all six of them for many years.

Our fun was keeping them all busy throughout the day. Lassen Pines was just down the road from us. They were glad to have Tom, Jim and Kaylynn come down every weekday morning and do some chores for them. Kaylynn helped in the camp kitchen and Tom and Jim worked with the janitor and maintenance man.

Debbie, Bob and Clyde did chores for us around the house each morning. Bob loved raking pine needles or shoveling snow in the yard. He and Clyde both cleaned horse corrals. Clyde really enjoyed the horses. Debbie we named "Little Dutch Cleanser". She loved dusting and vacuuming.

We gave all six of them spending money for doing their chores.

Randy graduated from Liberty Christian High School in June of 1984. He received a music scholarship to attend Western Baptist College in Salem, Oregon. He was greatly missed by all of us when he left.

About this time we experienced the most frightening experience we have ever had. It was a Sunday morning. We were sitting down to breakfast and noticed that Rusty was not with us. A quick search of the house and yard revealed he was definitely missing. Jim said that Russ had told him the night before that he was going to go to Bend, Oregon the next morning, but naturally Jim did not believe him.

We had a niece who had been working at Lassen Pines. She had gotten into some trouble and so she had left and returned to Bend. Rusty really loved her and had decided that he was going to go get her and bring her back. We should have paid more attention to him but we just did not. We had no idea how passionate he was about the situation. Now he and his bike were missing.

Steve took the car down the road and found Russ's bike alongside the highway just up from the camp. His heart went down to his feet. No sign of Rusty. No one at the camp had seen him.

It was a Sunday morning and we should all be leaving for church soon and Steve had to preach.

We called my parents (who lived in lower Shingletown) and they said they would start praying and help any way they could. Finally we called the sheriff. At first they said that since he was a sixteen year old they did not think they should be too alarmed yet. Steve informed him that he was mentally handicapped and this was out of character for him. They definitely needed to be alarmed.

Steve told me that until Rusty was found he did not know how he could preach. His mind was in a whirl. So he called Don Cole, the chairman of the church board, and asked him to please be prepared to do something for the morning service. Maybe they could read scripture, sing and have a prayer meeting. We averaged about 200 in attendance every Sunday so poor Don, he did not know what to do.

Then the sheriff came to the door. He was getting all the details about our runaway when the phone rang. It was the Redding Airport (which was over forty miles from our home). They said they had our son, Rusty, at the ticket counter. He was wanting to buy a ticket to Bend, Oregon with $2.00. And he was sobbing because he missed his Mom and Dad. Steve asked them to please hold on to him. Someone (probably his grandpa) would be there as soon as possible to get him. Steve talked to Rusty and told him Grandpa would be right down to get him.

With that news the sheriff left. We called Mom and Dad in lower Shingletown (about 15 miles closer to the airport than us). Dad said he would go right down and get him.

Don was sure happy with Steve's call that Rusty was found and that Steve could preach. But along with us he could not imagine how he had gotten all the way to the Redding Airport.

My Dad said that Rusty was sobbing when he picked him up and quietly sobbed the whole ride back in the car. When they passed a field of wild flowers he said, "Grampa, would you please stop so I can pick my Mom some of those flowers?" So Dad stopped and Rusty picked a little bouquet of wild flowers for me.

By then most of the church folk had heard the story. It was the middle of church when my Dad arrived with Rusty. He walked (still quietly sobbing) to the front near the piano(where he and I always sat) and handed me the little bouquet of flowers. The church folk did not know whether to laugh or cry. It was a day we will never forget.

Rusty at the ranch.

We never have figured out how he got to the Redding airport. He says that he got three rides. We think that three people were in the car that picked him up. We'll probably never know. But we were certainly thankful that it turned out well. And he never has run away again. It obviously was not a fun experience for him either.

I know I listened more carefully after that when any of the gang was upset about something. We sure did not want to go through something like that again.

Part V

Mountain Jewels Ranch, Little Valley

TWENTY-NINE

Mountain Jewels Ranch Little Valley

We began to realize we had two full time jobs. The church was growing and Steve was really busy studying for two Sunday messages and his Wednesday Bible Study.

He was also busy calling on new visitors and the sick folk. He did a lot of counseling. He had school board meetings and church board meetings.

We also had six handicapped young people as well as our own son Russ living in our home. Randy was attending Western Baptist College in Salem, Oregon. Heidi was such a help to us but was a busy ninth grader. She commuted each day to Liberty Christian School.

The ranch in Little Valley started to be more and more in our thinking as a possibility for Mountain Jewels Home. One day Steve gave John Bolesky, who was still living in Ohio, a call. Steve told John about our six new "kids" and asked if he still wanted a Christian ministry there in Little Valley. John told us yes, he definitely did and he seemed quite excited that we would be interested in the ranch for our "special family".

A few days later (on Steve's day off) we loaded the gang into the van and took an excursion to Little Valley. When we pulled into Little Valley, Steve and I looked at each other and said, "It's a good thing we called John before we came here to visit." It was more run down that we remembered.

We still really liked the cook house, the dance hall and the bunk house There were two homes in fairly good condition but the rest of the place was a mess. There was several old shacks that were rented out to folks. What a challenge we would have. Heidi said on the way home, "Mom I think it would be embarrassing to live there." Steve answered that it would definitely change quickly if we moved out there.

The ranch property in the valley was wonderful. There was two large ponds-one at the end of the valley and one over near Dixie Valley. The headquarters piece would take a lot of work but we could see it was a fantastic opportunity. It would certainly provide us with plenty for our six ranchers to do. It would allow for growth. And it was available for our use if we wanted it.

The next couple of weeks we prayed a lot and dreamed a lot. Then we made the decision to go for it.

Steve put in his resignation at the church. The church was so supportive.

We made plans to move to the ranch in June. In February Steve made a trip to Little Valley. He gave each of the folk that were living in the cabins a letter telling them that we would be moving to the ranch in June so they would need to be moving by the first of May. Most of the folk were nice but a few called Steve some really bad names. Steve was very kind and told them he was sorry but that we would be needing all the buildings. (He did not tell them that we would be burning most of them down).

There was one couple, Harvey and MaryAnn Lingo, that had lived there for years. Clover Corder (the daughter of Ned Bognuda, who was the original homesteader on the place) asked if we would consider allowing the Lingos to continue to live there. They had a single wide mobile home up on the corner of the ranch that they had added some rooms onto. Clover told us they were faithful with their rent and she thought they could be a help to us. She also thought relocating would be more of a problem to them.

Steve had a nice visit with Harvey and he felt very comfortable in telling them they could stay on. Harvey was overjoyed that they could stay. They turned out to be wonderful neighbors. They loved our "special ranchers" and were so good to them.

Shortly after we gave out the letters, one of our friends from the church in Shingletown came in to Steve's office to see him. He said that his son lived in Burney and had just heard a most interesting rumor. Someone had told him that a Rev. King was moving to Little Valley and was starting a commune called the Jewels People. (It was about the same time that the Rajneeshes were up in central Oregon.)

We enjoyed a good laugh over that rumor but decided it would be well to squelch it. So we went to the Mountain Echo (the local McArthur newspaper) and had them write an article on Mountain Jewels Home. They took pictures of the ranchers and wrote a nice article explaining what we were.

We sent letters to friends from North Valley Baptist Church and Grace Baptist Church in Redding and informed everyone at our church in Shingletown that we were going to have a big work retreat at the ranch over Memorial Day Weekend. We were going to burn several old buildings. We were going to paint the outside walls of the cook house, the lodge, the dance hall and two homes.. And we were going to do a lot of clean up work on the grounds. We invited them to come join us for the weekend. We asked that they bring campers or tents to sleep in. We would provide the food. They should bring work clothes and tools. Rakes and weed eaters would be quite welcome. And so would pickup trucks for trash pickup.

Two weeks before the big work weekend my parents and our good friends, Don and Bev Cole, and Steve and I went up to the ranch and scrubbed the cook house and the bunk house. The six of us scrubbed each day from dawn until dark and made those buildings ready for use. We stayed in the bunk house and had a great time of fellowship together.

Our sister-in-law. Christi, was living with us at the time so she stayed in Shingletown with the ranchers. Heidi was there to help her in the evenings.

We had about 30 folk show up on Memorial Day weekend prepared to work.

One man was a painter. He brought several paint spray guns. (We knew he was coming so had purchased a lot of paint). He sprayed all of the buildings that we were saving a dark brown. (We wanted a color that would cover up a "multitude of sins"). Some of the ladies followed him and painted the window frames a pale yellow.

Several folk brought lawn movers and weed eaters. Just mowing the weeds and raking the debris and trash around the cook house and the bunkhouse made such a difference.

We had a big truck and took numerous loads to the local dump. At that time there was no charge for the dump. We were afraid that it was our fault when they started charging at the Little Valley dump.

Some of the ladies brought sewing machines. We had bought plenty of fabric for curtains for the dining hall and the bunkhouse. The ladies made curtains and hung them in both of those buildings.

Another group of ladies scrubbed the windows, walls and floors in the bunkhouse, the cookhouse, and the three homes we left standing.

Some of the men burned down four of the old shacks. In a couple of the shacks they discovered bathtubs full of dirt with a sky light above them. The men laughed at me when I wondered what in the world that was all about. I found out they were the perfect arrangement for growing pot.

All that was accomplished that weekend was simply amazing.

We kept our home in Shingletown licensed and camped out at the ranch while we were getting the homes ready.

After several months we had the place ready for a State Licensing Inspection. The inspector was quite impressed with the set up we had there. God was so good. We were officially moved after that inspection.

Shortly after we moved to Little Valley we took in another girl, Julie Sunter. Julie had gone to school with Russ and Tom. Julie's Dad and Mom became friends of ours when the kids were in school together. .

Julie was a really vivacious fun girl but was a constant chatterbox.. The Lingo's were my life saver with Julie. She really loved Harvey and Maryann. They would have her over to play games almost every day right after lunch.

We also accepted another young man into our home —Tom Sowerby. Tom's parents were good friends of the Nicolet's (Debbie's parents). Tom had visited us several times over in Shingletown. He was a big guy, so we now had Big Tom and Little Tom. Our gang now consisted of five guys and three girls.

Steve and I lived in one of the houses we fixed up for the girls— Kaylynn, Julie and Debbie. Randy (who had taken a year off of college to help us) and Heidi stayed in the bunkhouse with Russ, Clyde, Big Tom, Little Tom, Bob and Jim. Randy was learning how to fly at the time. So many times in the evenings the guys all enjoyed sitting in their chairs in the bunkhouse pretending like they were in a cockpit taking off and landing, while Randy practiced talking to the flight controller.

Our girls, Debbie, Julie, and Kaylynn, in Heidi's home, 1988.

We ate all our meals together in the cookhouse. The cookhouse had a large kitchen. The dining room was large enough for us to have a dining area and a living room area. We had several long tables and benches in one area. At the other end we had a living room area with a large couch a couple of cozy living room chairs. That area also had a television and a nice carpet.

We could not get TV reception so we had a VCR player. Lots of folks made copies of the gangs favorite programs and we watched them in the evenings. Only a few times did we get to a real exciting place in the story and the tape ran out.

We watched Monday Night Football on Tuesday nights and we tried hard not to find out who won until we watched it. If anyone knew the winner they were not to tell.

The cookhouse was my favorite place. It had old wood siding inside and out and really is a unique cozy place. It had been built for the cowboys who worked on the ranch to eat in . There were two small rooms in the back of the dining area. We put a toilet and wash bowl in one of them and we used the other room for the office.

The kitchen had a big metal sink and a large gas cook stove that had six burners and a big oven. It also had a large griddle that Steve loved for making pancakes. He flipped many a pancake there.

I was so busy with the weed eater and other clean up jobs that Heidi often did the cooking. Jim named the kitchen "Heidi's Heavenly Hash House."

My brother Tom's church in Rancho Cordova sent a group of folk out for a work retreat shortly after we moved in. They put insulation in the roof of the cookhouse and the home that we lived in.

The Redding West Rotary Club came out one weekend and added another bathroom with a shower to the bunkhouse. That gave Steve and I a master bedroom suite in that home We had just moved into it.

They also plumbed the front entrance area so we could have a washer and a dryer in the bunkhouse.

Randy was off to college again. So Heidi moved into the other home with our three girls, Kaylynn, Julie and Debbie. (Heidi and Steve and I did a lot of switching those early days on the ranch).

The folk in the Fall River Valley were great to us. After one of Steve's first shopping trips to McArhur, he came into the cookhouse and announced to me, "I do believe we have just moved to the land of the Sacketts!" He had just met Rod and George McArthur (who tower over Steve's 6 feet). He had a really interesting chat with them and learned a little of McArthur history.

Doug Elzea came out a lot when we first moved and showed Steve how to flood irrigate the meadow. He helped him rebuild some of the ditches.

A doctor from Redding donated a tractor to us. The ranch still uses that tractor.

Don Hand gave us seven semmintal cows. One of them was a semmintal-brahma cross. Her name was Granny and she ruled the roost. Our fences all needed a lot of work so they often escaped (always with Granny in the lead). Those seven cows were the start of the MJR herd.

Wes Thompson, who was the pastor of the little church fellowship we attended, organized a community auction that raised $10,000 for the ranch.

We cleaned out the dance hall for a big recreation room. It had a basketball hoop in it that George Corder had used for years when he was a kid. The boys enjoyed shooting hoops out there. A few years after we were there, Jeremy MacFarland, a Fall River High School student, took our basketball area as his senior project. He sponsored a car wash and with the proceeds purchased a real nice basketball hoop and backstop

Winter on the ranch.

THIRTY

Life on the MJR

Excerpts from an article in the Mountain Echo on March 20, 1987 describes life at the ranch at that time. Randy had left for college. Steve's Mom, Grammy, and his sister, Pennie, were helping us that year.

Pennie moved into the home with Julie, Kaylynn and Debbie. Heidi lived with her cousins, Julie and Karen, in one of our other cottages. Grammy was living in the home that had been Clovers. Steve and I had all of the guys in the bunkhouse.

Ranch is a Home Full of Happiness

By Marty Burleson

Just beyond the Shasta county line in Lassen County exists the town of Little Valley, population 75. Its residents, whose fortunes died along with the town's decaying lumber mill, live mostly in trailers tucked back into the hills. The weathered Little Valley Café—like the other businesses in town—is a bordered up relic.

But just a hundred yards away, life exists. Here is a place with plenty of work and plenty of love. Here, as a fairy tale, adults seem never to grow old. They eat and work and laugh. They live.

The place is Mountain Jewel Ranch, a home for mentally handicapped adults, with emphasis on home.

Its eight "ranchers" as they're called sleep in a bunkhouse. They're called to dinner by the clang of a homey iron triangle. When they are not caring for cattle and horses on the ranch's 850 acres, they're enjoying hay rides, ping pong or video cassettes.

Just like home. Only better.

The proprietors of this sanctuary are Steve and Peggy King, parents of a mentally handicapped 19 year old.

The King's goal is to provide a place where the parents of mentally handicapped adults can turn a and a place where the mentally handicapped themselves can, in a "Christian atmosphere," be happy with their lives and their atmosphere.

Have they succeeded?

"We have fun times here together," said 34 year old Debbie Nicolet, a Mountain Jewel resident since 1983. "That's what I like."

Parents of the ranchers, most of whom come from Redding or nearby, are even more generous in their praise. Many have seen their children grow in self esteem.

"There isn't anything that compares with it in our opinion," said June Sunter, mother of 23 year old resident, Julie. "She's so happy there. It's a real family and that means a lot to us."

Others in the "family" are "Little Tom" Valles, 21; Clyde Lemos, 28; Bob Stark, 27; Jim Pinch, 28; Kaylynn Kinnier, 28; Tom Sowerby, 28; and the King's son, Russ. Running the show along with the King's are King's mother, Grammy, and sister, Pennie Black.

The King's daughter, Heidi, 17 and Pennie's daughter, Karen, 17, also live and help at the ranch.

According to the King's there are as many success stories at the ranch as there are ranchers.

Little Tom used to be a failure in school and would never shake hands. Now he will look you in the eye and shake your hand off.

Bob was afraid of animals. Today he raises rabbits and helps with the horses.

"This place has been a blessing for our son," says Joyce Stark, Bob's mother. "He wasn't growing with us. He was so dependent. It's amazing how much he has changed."

Recently, all the ranchers took a break from morning chores to tour the spread with visitors. Their exuberance was contagious. And their answers to the question, "What do you like most about the ranch?" were many.

"Horses," said Julie.

"Being out in the country," shouted Jim.

"Trips," chimed in Little Tom.

"Peggy," said Debbie with a blush while holding on to Mrs. King's arm.

Though they are adults it's tempting to call the residents "kids" because of their childlike nature and youthful appearance. That's childlike as in outgoing and eager, not as in ill-behaved.

There's a reason for that. "We do not take behavior problems because it would not be fair to the other residents." King said. "We feel it's important for each of our ranchers to fit into the family. We have to be real careful."

The Kings are currently trying to modify their license to accommodate 10 ranchers.- They are licensed by the State Department of Social Services, but King said that he is not anxious to fill beds. The determination to remain small comes despite the fact that word of the ranch has spread throughout the state, prompting some to suggest King "could have 50 ranchers in no time."

"We want to keep it family. We do not want to be big." Mrs. King insisted.

"We'd rather be parents than administrators'" King said.

The idea for the home came while Steve was pastor of the Open Door Community church in Shingletown. It began as a home for mentally handicapped children in 1983, The Kings began catering to adults once they realized there was a great need.

The group soon out grew the Shingletown facility. When a sprawling, run down ranch in Little Valley became available in 1985, King gave up his pastorate and snapped it up. Turning the crumbling buildings into a functioning ranch was a chore, as was winning over the local residents.

"When Little Valley heard we were coming they were all up in arms," Mrs. King said.

But now that they have met us and know us, they love us here."

Ed Plowright, chairman of the Little Valley Community Services district Board, confirmed the change of heart. "When we first heard about it there was a little hesitation," he said. "But since they've moved in, they've been accepted 100 percent. They're real good people and I've never heard a bad word about them."

Little Valley is not alone in embracing the ranch. Animals, a tractor, fencing and the labor to make most of the ranch building livable were donated by supporters. The Redding West Rotary Club makes frequent work visits and the Sun River Church in Rancho Cordova will participate in an old-fashioned barn raising on Memorial Day weekend.

"It's an excellent program," Redding West Rotary Club President Rob Long said. "We go up there and we don't want to leave."

The program also gets high marks from mental health experts. Lyn Pace, executive director of services for Intermountain Services for the Handicapped, said what's striking about the ranch is the happiness.

"As a body of people they're happy as bugs in a rug," he said. "There's joy. There's fun. You never see a frown on any of them."

Life at the ranch generally follows a regular schedule. The ranchers, who live in individual rooms decorated to their own tastes, rise for 8 a.m. breakfast. They clean their rooms before tackling chores—stacking firewood, feeding the animals.

Afternoons are devoted to such activities as basketball games, crafts, hikes and bowling on Thursdays. Once a week, a group of Little valley residents join the ranchers for a Bible Study.

Mealtimes may be the favorite part of the Mountain Jewel Ranch day.

Like a scene from "The Waltons" the crew happily gathers around a long, wooden table while King ladles out the soup de jour or whatever else "Grammy" and kitchen helper Debbie have cooked up. Conversation—about animals, the wind, and upcoming Special Olympics basketball tournament, anything and everything is non-stop.

Funding for the ranch comes from the ranchers Social Security checks, private donations, and family support. Twice a month, King distributes part of the Social Security income to the ranchers who save it for special occasions like dinners out, camping trips and once a year excursions. Such activities are important, King said, because while happiness may be the norm at the ranch, the mentally handicapped fight a constant battle against depression. The Kings help by keeping constantly "up" themselves.

"We were out once and somebody said, "Your group is always so happy." Mrs. King remembered. "Russ told them: 'It's the rules.'" According to parents and the Kings, nearly all of the ranchers are fated to a lifetime of supervision. But King doesn't see that as a tragedy.

"There's a freedom here. We can trust them and know that they are not going to go off somewhere," he said. "I know a lot of people punching a clock who wish they had that kind of freedom."

And the residents? Does the thought of spending the rest of their lives on this ranch bother them?"

"We joke about how we'll all look in 20 or 30 years." Mrs. King said to the accompaniment of much laughter. "I think we'll all grow old together."

The ranchers, smiling, Nodded in agreement.

Lunchtime in the Cookhouse, from left: Kaylynn, Grammie, Pennie, Jim, Tom, Clyde, Peggy, Steve, Russ, Debbie, Tom and Bob, 1987.

THIRTY-ONE

Family, Friends and Fire

There were so many people who helped us in those early days on the ranch that I am afraid to mention names. Dan and Martha Deaner helped a lot when we first moved to the ranch. We wanted to have them work with us full time but we realized shortly after we moved to the ranch that we did not have enough funding to support two families and improve the facilities.

Lee and Donna Cribbs helped us as house parents in Shingletown for a year.

Randy helped us all week and then worked weekends at KVIP radio station. On weekends he would stay in Shingletown with his Grandpa and Grandma McKee.

Heidi was a tremendous help.

Julie's Dad, Bob Sunter, was in charge of the area Special Olympics. He arranged for our gang to go to Lake Tahoe for the Winter Special Olympics. It was wonderful. They put us all up in a nice motel. The gang (including Heidi and Randy who went along as helpers) all got coaching from professional ski coaches. It was a real special week for all of us. We were able to go two years.

One day Heidi invited her best friend from Liberty Christian High School, Patty Prewett, to come up and visit her for a few days. She arranged for Randy to bring Patty up to the ranch after he got off work.

When Patty arrived with Randy, Heidi and I were cooking in the cookhouse. Patty came in and told Heidi, "Your brother is crazy!" Randy is a big tease, which she found out on the 60 mile drive from Redding to Little Valley.

During Patty's visit we noticed Randy was really enjoying her. He was always kicking her under the table. They started dating.

After the year that Randy took off from college to help us, he received a music scholarship to attend California State University Northridge. He came home to visit Patty several times that year. The next year Patty went to Masters College which is near CSUN. By that time they were engaged to be married.

Since Randy was a music major he sang in a couple of musicals each year. We were able to go down (all of us) for several of these performances.

One time that we went to southern California to see Randy, Tom Fox arranged for us to meet Roy Rogers at his museum in Apple Valley for a tour of the Roy Rogers Museum there.

We arrived early and were just arranging the whole gang around the big statue of Trigger for a picture, when a gentleman drove up in a small pickup. He had a baseball cap and tennis shoes on so we did not recognize him. He asked if he could get in our picture. I thought it a bit odd for this man to be asking to get in the picture but told him sure. Then he smiled and I recognized him. It was Roy! So we have a real nice picture of all of us in front of Trigger with Roy.

Then he said he had to change into his hat and boots and would give us a tour around. What a treat! He had his hound dog with him and asked him to sing for us. Roy sang a little song and when the dog was supposed to, he howled. It was great. Roy showed us around for awhile and then Dale joined us. Roy excused himself and went to his office. For the last half of the tour Dale showed us things. .

The MJR gang with Roy Rogers

Dale was so sweet and like Roy she treated us like we were their best friends. By then we had a lot of folk joining our group. As she showed us a lot of the mementos and pictures of their lives, Dale kept telling all of us, "This is just stuff folk. It is Jesus that counts."

We really appreciated them taking their time to show us around and treat us like we were really special to them. We were impressed by their gracious hospitality.

Heidi was able to be a housemother for our three girls, Debbie, Julie and Kaylynn her senior year. She was able to have a half day schedule.

Heidi was like a little mother on the school bus to many of the children from Little Valley. She carried rubber bands and a hairbrush (one she saved just for them) so she could brush their hair and fix them up a bit.

Heidi was chosen to go to Girl's State as the representative from FRHS and also went to the California Miss Teen Pageant. At the Miss Teen Pageant she won the Community Service award (cash and a trophy) which is given to the Miss Teen with the most hours of community service. She had over a hundred hours of service from helping with Special Olympics Basketball and Skiing. Julie's Dad, (Dr., Sunter) wrote a wonderful letter recommending her for the award.

We had taken the whole gang to the awards ceremony and had fun camping at the local KOA.

She graduated from high school in June 1988. She was salutatorian and so gave a speech. Randy sang, "Climb Every Mountain" at the graduation.

The next day was Randy and Patty's wedding. They had a lovely wedding at Grace Baptist Church in Redding. Heidi was a bridesmaid and Billy and Rusty were groomsmen. Don Ross, Randy's best friend, who was in his 70's, was the best man.

Tom and Barbara Fox had the music.

Randy and Patty moved down to Northridge where Randy was still in school.

Heidi started nursing school at Shasta College. During the week she stayed at my Dad and Mom's home in Shingletown and came home on weekends. We were really missing our Randy and Heidi.

Then came December 29, 1988.

John and Debbie Thompson, who had served as youth leaders for us at Open Door Church in Shingletown, and their two sons, had just arrived at the ranch with all of their belongings. They were going to be moving into the bunkhouse as house parents. They had moved a few boxes into the bunkhouse but most of their belongings were still in their trailer. They had gone to a wedding in Shingletown with us.

Steve and I had just moved out of the bunkhouse and down to the other ranch house. It was Christmas vacation . Heidi and I had spent the whole day before scrubbing the bunkhouse for the Thompson's move. We had waxed the floors and had given the bathrooms a real shine.

We had all returned from the afternoon wedding in Shingletown and were eating dinner in the cookhouse. Only Bob and Clyde had come back from Christmas vacation. The rest of the gang were still with their families.

Peggy and Billy at Randy's wedding

Randy and Patty's wedding, June 1988.

Out the window Steve noticed a red glow in the snow. He looked out and shouted, "The bunkhouse is on fire!"

He ran to the phone and discovered that the phone line was dead. Bob immediately started running out the door and up the road to our closest neighbors, Bill and Wendy Chuck's home. They were both on the Little Valley Fire Department.

While Steve and John did what they could with hoses, Heidi and I laid on the front porch and threw boxes of the Thompson's belongings (that they had unloaded there that morning) out of the building. We could not stand because of the smoke. It still amazes me that we were able to throw those boxes. Adrenalin really kicks in.

The fire department was finally able to extinguish the fire but by that time the whole building was gutted. After the fire crew left we all went to bed. We put the Thompson family in the home that Heidi had been living in. Heidi, Russ, Bob, Clyde and Steve in I slept in the other home (which Steve and I had moved into the day before). We found sleeping bags for Bob and Clyde.

Julie in her old bunkhouse room, 1987.

Old bunkhouse that burned to the ground.

I slept very restlessly and awoke about 3:00 a.m. and noticed the red glow again. This time the whole bunk house was totally engulfed in flames. I woke Steve and we went running up there. Steve rushed up to the Chucks home in Little Valley again and asked if they would bring a couple of fire trucks down to keep all the rest of the buildings safe. There was no sense in trying to save anything from the bunkhouse. It was a total loss. At this point letting it burn seemed the best option.

A few days later we heard that the rumor was going around Little Valley that we had set the fire to get the insurance money. We laughed at that rumor (however I must admit it did make me mad). We had a couple of insurance companies come out to give us an estimate on insurance and they simply refused to give us one. They said that because the buildings were so old and we were so far from adequate fire protection they would not insure them.

The Thompson's dog died in the fire. We think that he probably knocked some of the boxes that were stacked in the living room onto the gas floor furnace.

New home built after the fire

The morning after the fire I had the job of calling all the parents of the ranchers who were living in the bunkhouse (Clyde, Bob, little Tom, Kaylynn, and Julie) and telling them that the bunkhouse had burned along with all of their rancher's belongings. They were all shocked but assured us that they would start getting them fixed up. They were all so supportive and anxious to help however they could.

The day before the fire I had talked on the phone several times to MaryAnn Agee. Her son, Dennis, was coming down as a new "rancher" and was going to be moving into the bunkhouse. Mary Ann was getting a rug cut to fit his room and had called for the exact measurements. So I called her and said, "I sure hope that you haven't had the rug cut yet. The room is gone!" She couldn't believe it. Fortunately they had not cut it yet.

Well, once again God used a lot of great people to take care of us. The day after the fire our phone was ringing off the hook with good people inquiring how they could help.

There was an old building up in Little Valley that had seven bedrooms and a large living room and kitchen. It had served as a boarding house for mill workers and had been empty for several years. It was empty and the owner was very happy to rent it to us. It needed a lot of cleaning up. The folk from the Methodist church in Fall River Mills came out and spent a couple of days scrubbing the building and cleaning up the yard for us.

A lot of folk donated clothes for the ranchers who had lost everything. One church from Lookout bought new posters for each of the ranchers rooms and new CD's and videos. Many gave furniture to put in the lodge. People were so thoughtful and generous.

Having the group living up in the village of Little Valley worked but it was certainly not ideal. The gang came down to the ranch for lunch and supper. We were very anxious to rebuild but we had no idea how we were going to do it.

Our good friend, Jerry Boyle, was the president of the Redding West Rotary Club at the time. (They had recently added a nice bathroom on to the master bedroom in the bunkhouse that had just burned). He called and asked if they could help in anyway. We told him that we were going to have to build a new dorm home and could use any help we could get.

There was an architect in their group that volunteered to draw up plans for the new building. We sketched out what we wanted, which was basically the plan of the old bunkhouse with a kitchen and laundry room added to it. So he drew up the plans so that the building department would approve them.

Ralph Stearns, from the Rotary Club, was a building contractor who built a lot of large commercial buildings. He volunteered to send up some of his crews to help with each phase of the building.

A large crew from the Rotary Club came up and stayed for the weekend when the foundation was poured. After that Ralph sent up whatever crew was needed for the each phase.

Now all we had to do was raise the money for the building materials. Initially we were given enough money from our supporting churches to get us going. Then I started writing for grants.

I was excited to get a $10,000 grant from the Sierra Foundation. We kept getting enough gifts and grants to keep us building. After about a year we were able to move the gang all back to the ranch. We still had a lot of finish work to do.

Steve and I lived in the new dorm home with Debbie, Julie, Clyde, Bob, Russ and Dennis in the new dorm. Heidi lived with Big Tom, Little Tom and Kaylynn in the other home. She was a senior in high school and was able to have a half day schedule.

She enjoyed getting to drive our car to school each day.

Randy was attending Cal State University and majoring in music.

We fixed one of the cabins up for Jim. He was more high functioning than our other ranchers and had lived on his own for a long time. He has really enjoyed the independence. He still ate all of his meals with the rest of us. There were not kitchen facilities in his little cabin.

One day, shortly after we had moved into the new home, I was working at the sink and noticed a nicely dressed man drive up. I immediately thought, "Oh no, what kind of an inspector is this guy?" I reluctantly went out to greet him and was pleasantly surprised when he introduced himself as a representative from the Ben B. Cheney Foundation in Washington.

He told me that his foundation had gotten their start from little mills in the Fall River Valley. Then quite a few years ago they moved to Washington. They now were looking for a non-profit in the Intermountain area that had a need. He said that he had asked around the area and everyone he had talked to had suggested that Mountain Jewels Ranch might need some help. Well, I happily gave him a tour around the place and told him about the fire. Then I showed him what we needed to do yet in our new home.

They ended up giving us $10,000 for the new dorm home. That helped us complete the major project. God had certainly provided our needs through the gifts of so many wonderful people. The Cheney foundation helped us again several years later when we built the swimming pool.

THIRTY-ONE

A New Granddaughter and a Son-in-Law

After another year at CSUN Randy decided that what he really wanted to do in life was to fly. He was spending more time visiting airports then on his studies. So he and Patty moved to Macon, Georgia where he attended a flight school. While they were in Georgia, Rebecca Rose King (Becky) was born. We were so excited to be grandparents and could hardly wait to meet her.

As soon a Randy finished his flight training they moved into our Shingletown home. We had kept it licensed so we moved Kaylynn and the two Tom's over to that home. Randy started giving flight lessons in Redding.

Heidi attended Shasta College and took the nursing course. She stayed with my Dad and Mom in Shingletown each week, from Sunday afternoon until Friday morning, and came back home to help us on the weekends.

The summer after her first year at Shasta College, Heidi worked as a counselor for the junior camp at Mount Hermon which is near Santa Cruz, California. (We often took our whole gang there. We would camp at a nearby campground and then attend the morning and evening meetings.)

Heidi ready to leave for nurse's training at the hospital

During the counselor orientation everyone was asked to tell something about their self that was unique and unusual. Heidi related that she had been driving a car in the state of California for three years. She had driven hundreds of miles, since her home was over 50 miles from Shasta college. She stayed with her grandparents in Shingletown and commuted twenty miles to and from school each day from their place. Then she drove home to Little Valley each weekend. The unique thing was that in her three years of driving she had not once come to a stop light. (That was before Burney put their two stop lights in). That really surprised the city kids.

In her second year at Shasta College Heidi started dating Doug Williams. She met Doug while attending the Intervarsity Christian Fellowship club. She called me one day and told me that she had met a nice guy who wore cowboy boots.

Doug came up to the ranch several weekends and we really enjoyed his visits. He had always dreamed of someday working on a ranch for troubled boys. We hired him to help us. He was a big help to Steve, both with the guys and the ranch chores. He began leading the singing at our church.

Doug proposed to Heidi on what we now call "Engagement Hill" (a little hill at the end of the MJR meadow).

Doug and Heidi were married at the ranch on June 11, 1990. I'll never forget that day!

We mailed out a lot of invitations. We also put a wedding invitation in the church bulletin in Shingletown (where Steve was the pastor for nine years and Heidi had grown up). There was also an invitation in our church bulletin in Fall River Mills and in the church bulletin at Doug's home church.

I guessed that we just might have 250 people show up so we set up about 200 chairs that we had borrowed from church. Fortunately, we also set out a lot of hay bales for folk to sit on. The wedding was going to be behind the home that Heidi and Doug would be living in. It had a full view of the meadow.

We had church tables arranged under the trees in the grassy area we have alongside of the cookhouse. That has always been our picnic area.

It was a noon wedding and we were serving a pit barbecue beef dinner. We asked all the folk from our church to bring salads. I had bought a case of pork 'n beans. Steve's sister Judi had flown out a week before and had made a gorgeous huge wedding cake. And she had made a few sheet cakes.

Aunt Nancy made Heidi's wedding gown. She had made mine years before.

The night before the wedding we had the practice. Doug's parents, Denny and Carole Williams, had arrived with some of Doug's family. We had a wonderful rehearsal dinner that they provided.

Our neighbor, Ted Crum, is popular in our area for fixing pit barbecued meat. We had purchased close to 100 pounds of beef roasts. Ted and Duane dug a huge hole in the yard behind the cookhouse and had built a big fire in it the night before the wedding. About midnight it started to pour and it poured all night. I remember it vividly because Steve and I were sleeping in a tent. We had given our room to Steve's mother and sister, Pennie. I was so glad that we were in the tent and not some of our city guests.

I was watching the fire from the tent hoping that the rain would not extinguish it. And I was praying that the sun would shine for Heidi's wedding day. After watching the Crums bury all the meat in the fire pit, I fell sound asleep.

We woke to a beautiful day. Cowboys from our neighboring ranch, Dixie Valley, came on horseback to direct the traffic. The traffic started to come a little after 11:00 and it kept coming and coming. One man from Healdsburg said that he was afraid he would get lost but after leaving McArthur he just got in a line of cars and followed it for the next 18 miles.

Heidi and Doug's wedding.

Just before the wedding was ready to start, I was found rummaging in my desk for more paper to add to the guest book. They had run out of lines for the signatures. Steve said, "Honey, come. They're ready to begin!" I had just come from the Lingo's to see if they had a watermelon or something to cut up and add to the food. (We had asked all the folk from our church if they would bring salads). But we sure had a lot of people out there!

We looked down the road and there was Billy driving up the driveway. He had driven all the way out from Gallup and had arrived just in time. He said he would never miss Heidi's wedding.

Heidi looked beautiful and I thought the bride's Dad was extra handsome. My brother, Tom, married them. Rusty was a groomsman and Kaylynn was one of the bridesmaids. The bridesmaids all came in on the wagon pulled by Steve's Belgian team, Buck and Dolly. Our neighbor, Duane, drove the team for us. Then lastly, Doug, came in on Steve's Morgan stallion, Tuffy. Tuffy was excited and really pranced. They looked great. One person said that it reminded them of how it will be when the Lord comes on the Great Horse to claim His bride, the Church. Jim's job was to take Tuffy from Doug and lead him back to the barn.

Each of the gang had a part.

It was a beautiful wedding and everyone ate. But we sure did not have any leftovers. Judi said it was the first time she had served every piece of the wedding cakes.

Just as we waved to the bride and groom and they took off for their honeymoon, it started to pour. How thankful we were that the rain had waited until the party was over.

THIRTY-TWO

North to Alaska

A few weeks before the wedding Randy and Patty and little Becky had moved to Aniak, Alaska. Randy had obtained a job flying for Marc Airlines in Alaska. Aniak was way out in the Alaska bush country.

Randy was flying small planes from Aniak to the neighboring villages. He flew passengers, groceries and other supplies. His plane was also the sports bus that took the high school ball teams to the neighboring villages to play basketball. Patty was very pregnant when they moved up there.

Justin Randall was born on August 8 in Anchorage. Patty and Becky stayed with good friends, John and Mulholland, who lived near Anchorage, before and after Justin was born.

Marc Airlines flew jets from Anchorage into Seattle. We (Steve and I) were able to get tickets to fly from Seattle all the way to Aniak for just a few dollars because Randy was a pilot with Marc Air. We definitely took advantage of that. We purchased a regular ticket for Rusty. (It just made us thankful for the two almost free tickets we had.) We decided to visit them at Christmas because all of the ranchers would be home with their families. We were going to see Alaska and meet a new grandson!

Our trip was a great adventure. We flew on a big 747 from Reno to Anchorage. We arrived in the early afternoon and it was dark. We had to spend the night in Anchorage because there was not a flight to Aniak until morning. Fortunately we could fly on Marc Airlines planes all the way to Aniak.

The next morning we took a smaller jet to Bethel. When we were arriving in Bethel the captain announced, "Welcome to Bethel! The wind is blowing at 80 knots and the temperature is 40 degrees below zero." Brrr! When we stepped off of that plane I couldn't believe it. I had never felt such cold.

It was so cold that we had to wait until it got warmer to take the small plane out to Aniak. Randy explained that they can not take off until it has warmed up to about 20 degrees below. So we sat at the Bethel airport for several hours. There is not much to see at the Bethel airport. Actually there was not much in the town of Bethel. Randy said that there is one bush that has grown in Bethel and they are very proud of it.

Finally we climbed aboard a smaller plane and headed to Aniak. We still did not see much because it was dark even though it was just after noon.

Randy met us at the airport in Aniak. He loaded us and all our gear on his snowmobile and a toboggan pulled behind it. I sat on the toboggan with the gear as we whizzed over the trails through the rustic village to their little home. By 3:00 p.m. it was pitch dark again.

It was fun to hold our first grandson, Justin, and to play with little Becky. She was 22 months old.

Randy had found a sad looking little tree to decorate for Christmas. By the time he pulled it home with the snowmobile it had three leaves left on it. We had quite a laugh over that. But when the Christmas decorations were put on the naked branches, it was really quite cute. I can still see it in my mind's eye. An ordinary tree would have probably left my mind by now.

The next day was Sunday so we loaded onto their snowmobile and a trailer to go to church. (There were hardly any automobiles in the village). I was on the toboggan trailer, snuggled in a sleeping bag with one year old Becky. It was so cold Becky and I snuggled deep into the bag. We whizzed to church with Randy driving. When we got there Randy wanted to know how I enjoyed seeing the village. I let him know that I had not seen a thing. Becky and I were buried in the bag. It was much too cold for this Californian to peak my head out. It was also still dark.

We had a great time and really enjoyed their new friends up there. The pastor of their little church was Terry Bissonette. He was just two years behind us at Biola College so knew a lot of the same people.

Terry and his wife, Debbie, had taken our kids into their hearts and home and were wonderful to them. We felt like they were family. Terry was the village magistrate, which was like a judge. He loved to hunt and fish so Aniak was a perfect fit for him.

We were shocked at the price of food. Everything has to be flown in from Anchorage. Patty was making her own bread because it was close to $6 for a loaf and often it was stale. Meat and produce were not fresh and terribly expensive. Whenever someone "went out" (that was what a trip to Anchorage was called), they took at least one large ice chest so they could bring back fresh milk, meat, and produce. After that first visit we brought an ice chest full of meat and produce with us every time we made a trip up.

On our return journey Patty and the kids flew back with us. Patty's family were anxious to meet Justin and see Patty and Becky again. It was fun having them with us on our flights and we were glad that we could be a help Patty. A baby and an 18 month old can be a real handful to travel with.

A few months after Patty and the kids returned to Alaska, we got a very frightening call from Randy. Justin was deathly ill. He had suddenly gotten so he hardly moved. He did not want to eat and seemed to have no energy to try do anything. Justin had been a very active baby.

Patty had to fly him to Anchorage to see a doctor. It was discovered that he had infant botulism. He needed to be in the hospital. The doctor said that when Justin had the strength to open his eyes and close his mouth he would be well enough to go home.

Once again John and Debbie Mulholland took Patty into their home. She had little Becky with her. We were so glad that Patty's Mom, Linda, was able to fly up and stay with Becky at the Mulhollands while Patty went to the hospital each day.

With a full week of hospital care and lots of prayer Justin healed and was soon his active self again.

THIRTY-THREE

Trips

Some of our favorite memories with our gang are of the many trips we took together. Steve and I always enjoyed camping with our family so as our family grew we just had to be more innovative on planning the trips.

Early on we began taking the gang to Mt. Hermon each summer. We would camp at Henry Cowell Redwoods State Park, which was just a few miles down the road from Mt. Hermon. Then we would attend the morning and evening services that Mt. Hermon provided. It worked great.

Heidi and I would fix easy meals. And we would go to the local MacDonald's a couple of times a week. . Once we even had the local pizza place deliver a couple large pizzas to our campsite for a special treat.

We would have to get two campsites to hold all of our little tents. Most of the ranchers had their own tent. Several liked to share because sleeping out in the woods made them a bit nervous. We usually had a lot of small yellow dome tents. .

Dennis was a riot. He thought sleeping on the ground in a tent was the dirtiest thing he could think of. So in the morning he was usually found sleeping in the van. It struck us funny that he thought it was dirty because Dennis was our rancher who hated to wash.

The campground was only a few miles from Santa Cruz, so we always spent some time on the beach. Mt. Hermon offered a train ride on the narrow gauge railroad from Felton to the Santa Cruz Boardwalk. We took that trip several years with the gang.

The conference had wonderful speakers and music. We always sat up front and made many new friends.

Jack Pearson, known as the Song Singing Story Man, became a great friend. He was so sweet and special to the guys. He makes up the greatest stories and songs. Twice we had him come to our church in Fall River and give programs, which he does full time during the winter months. He and his wife, Nancy, came and visited us a couple times at the ranch and Jack did a concert for us at our church.

We met our rancher, Todd Cerf, through Jack and Nancy.

One summer we took the gang to Broken Arrow Bible Camp (our New Mexico home). On the way to the ranch we stayed at the Grand Canyon Motel and took a train ride to the Grand Canyon. The train ride was great.

Our good friends, Dr. Al and Sheila Diddams, who now live near Sedona, Arizona, came up and had a meal with us at the motel buffet. We had a wonderful reliving so many memories and catching up on each others families and lives.

We went the end of August, so that the camps were just over at BABR. It was really great for our gang to get to be a real help cleaning up after a summer of camps.

Tom and Scott enjoyed helping and cleaning with me in the kitchen. Chad and Rusty cleaned and organized the sports equipment closet at the recreation area and the Bibles and song books in the chapel.

Doug, Ryan L. and Justin cleaned out a big closet in the bottom of the dining hall building and shampooed a couple of rugs.

Bob, Ryan Y. and Michael helped chop and stack fire wood.

Heidi, Scott, Tom and I worked in the kitchen. We cleaned out the pantry and the walk in freezer. And helped with the meals.

Steve helped shoe the horses.

Billy's sister, nieces, and Mom with the MJR crew at her home in New Mexico.

One afternoon we took the guys way out onto the reservation to visit Billy's family. Billy's Mom still lives in the small hogan she lived in years ago. She and Billy's sister and nieces live way out on a sandy dirt trail. She was so sweet and invited all of the guys into her home. It is very rare to get invited into a hogan.

Billy's niece had a baby girl that the gang was all enjoying. While Michael was playing with the baby, she laughed for the first time. Navajos have the custom to give candy and have a party at the time of the baby's first laugh. So Billy's niece went running into her little home (which was a small cabin) and brought out pieces of candy for all of us. That was really special. Michael still talks about making the baby laugh.

I was especially thrilled when Billy's Mom gave me a big hug when we were leaving and said in her broken English, "Thank you for you do Billy." I gave her a big hug back and we both shed some happy tears.

We had a great time with the staff there. It was especially fun for Steve and I to see how well things were going there.

On the way home we camped at Needles, California. It was over 100 degrees when we arrived for the evening. I had planned to fix hot dogs, but it was so hot there was no way I wanted to cook hot dogs.

After leaving the guys with Doug and Heidi to set up camp, Steve and I went to a store and bought a bunch of fruit for a salad. Then we went back to the KOA and joined everyone else in their swimming pool.

We all slept on top of our sleeping bags that night.

THIRTY-FOUR

Building a New Home a New Grandson and A Diary in *Farm and Ranch Living Magazine*

We had six ranchers in the new home we had built after the fire. Jim had his own little cabin. Doug and Heidi had Kaylynn and the two Toms in their home. Ten ranchers was full capacity for us.

Life settled into a good routine. We had breakfast in our own homes and lunch and dinner all together in the cookhouse. Heidi an I took turns with the cookhouse meals.

We had rented the other small home to Duane and Sam Crum. The Crums who owned the property, around our headquarters piece. The Crums owned the first third of the meadow and we had the rest.

We were wanting to build Doug and Heidi a large home. One with room for their MJR ranchers and room for a family. The best spot was right where the old home was that we were renting to Duane and Sam.

Duane really liked that home. His uncle had helped build it years before. So we came up with the idea to give them the home if they would just move it. They thought that was a great plan. So house movers jacked it

Doug and Heidi's new home at MJR

up and moved it over to Crumbs property. They added on to the home and made it really nice.

Heidi and I found a nice looking two story ranch style home in a magazine and ordered the plans for it. It had a large front porch. We made a few changes (like making the garage into two more bedrooms and a bathroom for a couple of ranchers. There was another large bedroom and bathroom downstairs.

Doug and Steve started work on it. Phil Dabill, a carpenter who went to our church, came out every morning and would work with them for a few hours. He was their coach but they built most of the home.

Once again we got a lot of help. The Burney Rotary club helped a lot. The area mills gave us a good deal on the lumber. Hat Creek Construction helped with septic tank and the foundation. And many helpers from our supporting churches came out and helped.

The new home overlooks the meadow and was a wonderful addition to the ranch. Now all of our ranchers were in new homes (except for Jim who was so excited about having his own cabin). We had never anticipated that just a few years before.

Shortly after Doug and Heidi moved into their new home with their ranchers, Dusty was born. What a joy it was to have a grandson right on the ranch.

About that same time we decided that the time had come to move my parents closer to us. My Mom's parents had both passed away so Dad and Mom were no longer needed in Shingletown. Dad's health was not real good. They were excited that they could move the mobile home on to the ranch that had been my grandparents. So Grandpa and Grandma McKee joined us on the ranch.

The next year Marc Airlines went bankrupt and Randy was out of a job. He moved his family down from Alaska into the home that had been vacated by Doug and Heidi. Never a dull moment!

Randy flew a crop duster for the summer. Then he got a job working at the local John Deere Equipment store.

Shortly after Randy moved down, Doug and Heidi, gave us a third grandson, Brad. He was a year and a half old when I wrote the following diary for the Farm and Ranch Living Magazine. It follows life on the MJR for the entire month of February 1998.

NINE SPECIAL HANDS DO the WORK on THIS RANCH

PROFILE: Steve and Peggy King operate Mountain Jewel Ranch near Little Valley, California with their daughter and son-in-law, Heidi and Doug Williams. They raise beef cattle and Morgan horses and grow hay on 900 acres. More importantly they care for nine mentally challenged adults-one their son- whom they call "ranchers". Peggy kept this diary.

FEB. 1: Welcome to Mountain Jewel Ranch. We're located in beautiful Little Valley in the northeastern corner of California. Steve and I moved here with our family 13 years ago with a dream of starting a special type of ranch. One of our sons, Russ, has Down's syndrome and we felt this lifestyle could be beneficial. Now we're a licensed Adult Residential Facility.

Our daughter and son-in-law, Heidi and Doug Williams, and their sons, Dusty, 4, and Brad, 1 ½, live here too. As do my parents, Bill and Virginia McKee. So there are four generations on this "home on the range".

Then there's our extended family of eight mentally challenged adults, Mark Welch, Debbie Nicolet, Dennis Agee, Clyde Lemos, Jim Pinch, Bob Stark, Tom Valles and Ryan Young. Together with our son, Russ, we call them our nine "ranchers". You'll get to know them better throughout this month.

We're especially thankful to our dear friends, John and Joyce Bolesky, who own the ranch. They generously deeded the ranch headquarters site over to us and give us free use of the rest of their 900 acres, enabling us to fulfill our dream of providing this fantastic life-style for our family and ranchers.

Before we came here Steve was a pastor in nearby Shingletown. That's where we started gathering our extended family. All of our ranchers come from wonderful families, and we've become great friends with their parents.

We run about 60 head of cows and put up 400 tons of grass hay each summer. Steve raises Morgan horses and also has a team of Belgians, "Buck" and "Dolly". Most of our ranchers have an animal project so we also have pigs, rabbits, chickens, a donkey and a ewe."

Doug and Heidi work full-time with us and keep their ranchers at their house. The other six live in our home. Patty works part-time as a relief housemother and helps take care of the ranchers when we're away.

This morning while Steve was out doing chores, I roused the gang and got them headed to church by 8:30. We attend the Intermountain Evangelical Free Church in Mcarthur, about 20 miles north of here.

After lunch, Steve took Ryan and Bob- two of our

Like Salt & Pepper

Steve raking hay with Buck and Dolly.

ranchers who never miss a chance to go to the field- out to feed the cows. They came back with news that one of our Simmental cows had a nice heifer calf this morning.

FEB. 2: We had French toast and fruit for breakfast. Then every one went off to do chores 'till noon. Steve, Doug, Bob, Jim, Ryan and Dusty hitched the Belgians to the hay wagon and fed the cows. Russ cleaned the van.

Mark cleaned horse stalls in the barn. Tom and Debbie helped Heidi and me with some of the housework while Dennis tackled a big pile of laundry.

It's Heidi's day to cook. She cooks lunch and dinner for the whole gang on Mondays and Tuesdays, and I cook for everyone on Wednesdays and Thursdays. We each cook for our own households the other 3 days. That gives each of us 2 days off.

FEB. 3: Tuesdays is our regular bowling day. I took the gang to Burney—a 45 mile drive- to bowl with the Special Education Classes from the Burney schools and the Intermountain Services for the Handicapped. Tom was our high point man today.

Steve and Clyde hauled a truckload of hay to a feed store in Redding that buys a load from us every week. On the way back, Steve picked up a log bed that we ordered from a friend before Christmas. I can't wait to get it sanded, finished and set up in our bedroom!

FEB. 4: I took my mother and Debbie to Redding. Debbie is our only female resident and enjoys having a "ladies day out" with us.

Steve, Doug, and Jim (one of our highest-functioning ranchers, who is able to ride by himself) worked cattle. Later, Doug shod "Toby", one of our Morgan horses.

FEB. 5: It rained today. At an elevation of 4,200 feet, we usually have snow this time of year. We sure aren't used to al this mud! Russ has been sinking to his ankles in mud when he feeds his two pigs, named "Breakfast" and "Dinner".

Doug drove the guys to basketball practice. Every Thursday from January through March, the Fall River High School Leadership Class helps our rancher team practice for the Special Olympics Basketball tournament.

Dusty tagged along with Steve to check the cows and drop off some protein and mineral supplement in each of the three pastures. They returned in time for Steve to work a couple of his Morgans in harness.

FEB. 6: It's still raining, and the weatherman says we can expect more, thanks to El Nino.

Most of the gang did indoor jobs. Russ helped me sand the log bed to get it ready for finishing. Tom, Dennis and Debbie had their usual cleaning chores.

Mark shelled walnuts, and Clyde chopped wood in the shed. Ryan, Bob and Jim bundled up in slickers and went with Doug to feed the cattle.

The guys were excited this morning because a friend

from the highway patrol stopped by. He gave them a short ride around the ranch in his patrol car.

FEB. 7: Saturday is cleaning day for the ranchers- each of them has their own bedroom.

Steve hitched up Buck and Dolly to feed cattle, and Justin and Becky rode along in the wagon. This afternoon Steve worked several young horses in harness.

I did some serious housecleaning and fixed a big pot of chili and cornbread.

FEB. 8: Sunday. Granddaughter, Becky, is 8 years old today. We have five birthdays on the ranch in February. We attended church this morning.

After supper, the gang gathered around the television and watched the Winter Olympics.

FEB. 9: We woke up to snow this morning- so beautiful and much better than mud.. Doug, Ryan and Dusty trucked a load of hay to Redding.

Steve hitched up the team to the hay wagon and took several of the guys with him to feed the cows. The cows are about a mile and a half from our headquarters, so feeding them is time-consuming. But the ranchers think it's great.

Mark, who has Down's Syndrome, put it well as he crawled into bed tonight, "I love my life," he said.

FEB. 10: Doug and Heidi took the crew bowling. Afterward, they went out for Chinese food.

I put a second coat of finish on the log bed, then drove Jim, Mark and Ryan to McArthur to do grocery shopping. They chose not to bowl today.

We stopped at the John Deere Dealership to see son Randy, an equipment salesman. Randy was a bush pilot in Alaska for 5 years, and we're glad to have him and his family home again.

FEB. 11: Steve, Becky and Clyde took a load of hay to Shingletown.

Happy Birthday, Debbie! She moved in with us when she was 30, and today she is 45. For her birthday dinner, she chose enchiladas, tossed salad, refried beans and chocolate cake with chocolate frosting.

FEB. 12: Doug and the guys went to the high school for basketball practice. While they were gone, Steve and I set up the log bed. It really adds a nice "ranch look" to the bedroom.

After lunch, Steve and Doug sorted out six cows to take to the auction tomorrow. Steve and I hauled a bale of hay out to them with the six wheeler after supper. The sunset over the meadow was gorgeous.

Doug and Randy had a Flying Sheriff's Posse meeting tonight. Doug's a pilot, too, and they are both officers in the group, which is occasionally called upon for aerial searches.

FEB. 13: Steve left at 5:30 a.m. to take the cows to the auction. Ryan and Clyde rode along. Clyde never misses a chance to ride in the truck—his dad is a truck driver, and Clyde loves truckin'.

I packed for a weekend trip. Steve and I are driving my parents to Los Gatos for the 50th anniversary celebration of the church they helped start. They're pretty excited, and I am too- I'll see lots of folks I grew up with.

FEB. 14: Saturday! We left at 6 a.m. for Los Gatos and ran into rain, hail, lightning, fog and sunshine. The weather changed so fast that Steve said it reminded him of the man who slipped on the ice, fell in a mud puddle and then got up and dusted himself off!

FEB. 15: Sunday. We attended a wonderful 50th anniversary church service in Los Gatos. A 200 voice choir sang the "Hallelujah" chorus. There were more people in the choir than we have in our entire congregation!

It was a great trip. But we're always thankful to return to our home on the range. We arrived about 8:30 p.m. and the gang had a lot to tell us.

FEB. 16: It's raining again. The corrals are so muddy that Steve moved several of the horses to the meadow.

FEB. 17: Happy 30th birthday to our son Russ!

His birthday brings back lots of memories to Steve and me. When we discovered he had Down's Syndrome, someone rightly told us, "Trials are just opportunities to prove God's faithfulness." Russ has been a real joy and led us to our work on the ranch.

After a birthday dinner of spaghetti, tossed salad, garlic twists and lemon meringue pie, we all went to the high school basketball game. Fall River won again—and if they win their last game on Saturday, they'll make the playoffs.

FEB. 18: Steve and Doug loaded hay for a haul to Shingletown tomorrow.

Our hay ground is flood irrigated natural meadow grass, timothy and clover. We start haying the first of July and usually finish in mid-August.

Doug usually operates the swather. Ryan, Jim and Russ are able to drive the tractor to do the raking. Steve runs the baler and usually bales from late afternoon until midnight. Then Doug picks up the bales with the accumulator from late afternoon until midnight.

They all enjoy haying, but by the time they're finished, they're glad we have only one cutting.

FEB. 19: Steve left for Shingletown at 5:30 a.m. with the load of hay. This afternoon a little heifer calf was born. Later, it started snowing again.

FEB. 20: I did some bookwork, then went to McArthur to pick up medicine for my dad. He'll be 85 soon and is not in good health.

Fortunately, Heidi is a registered nurse and can give him shots.

The California Department of Social Services, which licenses our facility, is glad we have a nurse on our staff since we live way out here.

FEB. 21: Saturday. Steve battled snow to feed the cows. He returned with sad news that coyotes had killed a new-born calf. He'll move our donkey down to the pasture- she does a great job of chasing off coyotes.

Fall River won their basketball game. Next stop is the playoffs. Our gang sure were excited.

FEB. 22: Sunday. The ride to church was beautiful with all the new snow. But we're praying for the California farmers—the soil is so soggy that they can't get into their fields to plant and the weatherman is predicting another 3 months of rainfall.

FEB. 23: Steve, Patty, Justin and Becky saddled their horses and rode out to check on the new calves. The calves and their mamas were doing fine.

FEB. 24: Today was a great day for several reasons. First, the sun was shining. Second, it was Doug's birthday. We're thankful for such a loving, helpful son-in-law.

There was also a Bowling Tournament for the handicapped bowlers in the area. It included a luncheon at the bowling alley and nice prizes for each of the participants, thanks to donations from the community businesses. Our gang had a great time.

FEB. 25: Steve, Ryan and Clyde delivered a load of hay to Redding. The rest of the ranchers helped Doug with chores. They came back with news that we had three new calves last night- a bull and two heifers.

Doug, Jim and Bob repaired fence. Why is it that our cows always want out and the neighbor cows want in?

Tonight was the first playoff game and Fall River won! The guys were really excited.

FEB. 26: Steve left early to deliver another load of hay. When he returned home he put up a temporary fence to give Russ's pigs some "dry" ground. With all the rain their pen was becoming a mess.

I took Debbie to McArthur for a doctor's appointment. Later, we did the grocery shopping.

FEB. 27: All of the calves born this week are a reminder that it won't be long before spring branding. The ranchers take part in branding day, and many of our friends come to watch. I haul a huge lunch down to the corral and serve it tailgate-style right off the pickup.

It was a beautiful day, so Mom, Debbie and I took a walk after lunch. It was a welcome break for me because I had spent most of the morning getting tax records ready for our accountant.

FEB. 28: Saturday. Today is Mark's birthday, which is a miracle. He has a severe heart defect and wasn't expected to survive infancy. But he is one of our most active ranchers.

Thank you for letting us share our lives with you this month. We'd love to have you stop by for a visit if you're ever up in this beautiful country. Good bye and God bless you!

Peggy King

MJR Family photo taken at Mt. Hermon in 2002. Bottom Row: Marilyn, Chad, Peggy, Ryan L., John, Ryan Y., Mark, Dusty, and Brad. Top Row: Jim, Bob, Justin, Russ, Steve, Scott, Tom, Doug and Heidi.

THIRTY-FIVE

Lots of Wonderful Help

So many volunteers helped to make Mountain Jewels Ranch the beautiful place that it is. One family stands out as having worked on every project we have had since we met them. They are the Schneider family from Placerville and Shingle Springs.

One day we were all eating in the bunkhouse when some hunters came to the door to use the phone. One of them was particularly interested in our gang and wanted to know our story. He said that his family had a construction business. They bought old houses and fixed them up and then sold them. They were very experienced in all aspects of the building business. He told us that any time we needed help to give them a call and they would be up.

We had recently hired Marilyn Jacobson to be our cook. Steve and I had met Marilyn and her family years before and had kept in touch. Heidi and I needed relief from some of the cooking chores so we had contacted Marilyn. Marilyn has been a tremendous help both as a cook and a relief housemother. She loves the guys and they love her.

Marilyn had just moved into the home that all of us had lived in one time or another. It needed a lot of work.

It did not have a foundation and was rotting. The front porch was falling off. The walls were crooked.

The Schneider family has worked wonders with that home.

They also came and helped add an addition on to the large dorm home. It enabled us to have another rancher by moving Russ into the addition and added a beautiful master bedroom and some pantry storage.

They just recently added on to Doug and Heidi's home and totally remodeled the kitchen. They turned a tiny little kitchen into one that is gorgeous and first class. It was greatly needed.

I hate mentioning names because the Mountain Jewels Ranch has been built and continues to operate because of the gifts and help by volunteers. We thank you everyone for your efforts in this ministry.

MJR Gang in 1994

THIRTY-SIX

Grandchildren and the MJR Wranglers

Steve and I had often laughed at our friends who always wanted to talk about their grandchildren. We were not going to be that way. And then we got some. We did not realize how special everyone of them is to a Grandpa and Grandma.

Randy and Patty had already given us Becky and Justin. Heidi and Doug had little Dusty. Then three years later Brad came along. And a few years after that Randy and Patty had Jessica and a year and a half later they had Callie. So we have six wonderful grandkids.

When Dusty was eight he started taking fiddle lessons with Trisha Ferguson in Redding. Brad was just five and started taking the guitar from her. It was amazing how they took to those instruments at such a young age. (Now I really am sounding like a proud grandma.)

Every morning (Monday through Friday) Dusty would walk up to our home with his little fiddle and I would play his pieces with him. We practiced a half an hour every week day. It was such fun. We both really enjoyed it. I was excited because I had always wanted to learn the fiddle tunes.

The MJR Wranglers: Justin, Brad, Becky, Peggy and Dusty

Before long he was entering fiddle contests and doing quite well. Brad practiced hours on his little guitar and also started entering the picking contests. Both boys really loved their music.

Becky was playing the piano and thoroughly enjoyed it. She also practiced a lot each day. Then Justin took up the violin. And the Randy King family moved back down to our area.

We really started having fun playing together. We formed a group we now call the MJR Wranglers. Justin, Dusty, and I on the fiddles. Brad on the guitar. We got Becky a big string bass and with her piano background she picked up plucking the bass notes right away.

Our first concert was for the annual luncheon that the Fall River Garden Club gives for all the shut ins in the area. We became their annual entertainment and they have watched the kids grow up not only physically

Like Salt & Pepper

but on their instruments. This past spring we played at their luncheon for the seventh year. They have been a wonderful encouragement.

We have played every year at the Frontier Days at Burney Falls. And we played at the annual Museum Days in Fall River until Little League games started conflicting with that date. The last few years we have played at the Intermountain Fair.

Now we have lost Becky and Justin to college. Dusty has only two more years before he leaves. Doug started playing the bass guitar and is playing Becky's part. This year Brad was on a trip so we added son Randy on the guitar and my brother Tom on the banjo for eight one hour concerts at the Intermountain Fair.

Life goes on!

Grandma and Grandpa with Callie, Becky, Dusty Justin, Brad and Jessica

THIRTY-SEVEN

The Journey West

And life continues to go on daily at Mountain Jewels Ranch. The ranch has been home to over twenty very *special people*. *And many wonderful people* have given of their time, talents, and energy to make it all possible. And they continue to do so.

In August 2006, Steve and I decided that it was time for us to leave the ranch in the capable hands of Doug and Heidi. We had started the home in 1983 in Shingletown and had been in Little Valley for twenty one years. If we were going to give them the reins we better get out of the way and let them do it.

Our son Randy found us a really neat place that we could rent in Cassel called Hidden Valley Ranch. We can walk to Randy's home from it. The home has a nice little home adjacent to it that was available for my Mom. The property has a large old barn, corrals, a meadow, two ponds and a big garden spot. So we made plans to move there.

We moved most of our belongings and all of Mom's to our new homes in Hidden Valley Ranch by conventional means. Then Steve hitched Tiny and Too Tall (our two Belgian draft horses) to a wagon for the last leg of our journey. It seemed like the best way to move the big wagon and those two huge draft horses. And we had been dreaming of taking a trip by wagon for some time. Now was the time.

We wanted to leave in the evening so we could make the big climb out of the valley while it was still cool. Then the horses could rest after the climb while we had a good nights sleep.

So we rode out of the MJR entrance gate into the sunset.

Epilogue

Steve always has a story, a poem or a joke for every occasion. So I asked him the other day how I should end our story. He answered, "Let me think about it."

The next morning he said, "Why not end our story with one of my favorite poems, 'Drinking From My Saucer' "

I was so excited. It fits.

DRINKING FROM MY SAUCER

By John Paul Moore 1970

I've never made a fortune and it's probably too late now,
But I don't worry about that much, I'm happy anyhow.
And as I go along life's way I'm reaping better than I sow,
I'm drinking from my saucer 'Cause my cup has overflowed.
Haven't got a lot of riches and sometimes the going's tough,
But I've got loving ones around me and that makes me rich enough.
I thank God for His blessings and the mercies He's bestowed,
I'm drinking from my saucer
Cause my cup has overflowed.
O, I remember times when things went wrong
My faith wore somewhat thin,
But all at once the dark clouds broke
And sun peeped through again.

So Lord, help me not to gripe about the tough rows that I've hoed,
I'm drinking from my saucer "Cause my cup has overflowed"
If God gives me strength and courage
When the way grows steep and rough,
I'll not ask for other blessings I'm already blessed enough.
And may I never be too busy to help others bear their loads,
Then I'll keep drinking from my saucer
"Cause my cup has overflowed."